ESTABLISHED IN 1973

PUBLISHED QUARTERLY
by Berea College
CPO 2166
205 N. Main Street
Berea, KY, 40404

Telephone: 859.985.3559
Facsimile: 859.985.3903
Email: appalachianheritage@berea.edu
www.appalachianheritage.net

 Periodicals postage paid at Berea, Kentucky, and at additional mailing offices. ISSN# 03632318.

The short stories in this publication are works of fiction. Names, characters, places, and incidents are either the products of the authors' imaginations or are used fictitiously. Any resemblance to actual events, locales, or persons, living or dead, is entirely coincidental. The views expressed in the creative nonfiction herein are solely those of the authors.

Electronic submissions only at www.appalachianheritage.net

Distributed by the University of North Carolina Press. Basic subscription price: $30/year for individuals, $40/year for institutions. For subscription requests and inquiries, visit the magazine's website, email uncpress_journals@unc.edu, or call 919.962.4201.

CONTENTS

EDITOR'S NOTE

JASON HOWARD

In 1953, William Styron was riding high on the success of his debut novel, *Lie Down in Darkness,* which had been published two years earlier to great acclaim. He was just twenty-eight when he sat down with Peter Matthiessen and George Plimpton at a café on the Boulevard Montparnasse in Paris for an interview that appeared in the spring 1954 issue of *The Paris Review*. It's easy to imagine the young Styron there, sipping an Americano, and musing about what qualifies as good literature. "A great book should leave you with many experiences, and slightly exhausted at the end," he said. "You live several stories while reading it."

Over sixty years later, Styron's proclamation continues to ring true. However, I would modify it to apply to shorter creative works as well—to short stories, creative nonfiction, and poetry—and indeed, to the writing that appears in this issue of *Appalachian Heritage*. With that, dear readers, you have been given fair warning: you will reach the end of this issue having inhabited several lives and visited many places, including a courtroom, a diner, an Intensive Care Unit, a dive gay bar replete with Whitney Houston drag queens, a junkyard, an amateur animal sanctuary, and an art gallery to name but a few. You may close the back cover with a sheen of sweat on your brow, in need of a stiff drink. But you will have lived.

You will be guided on this journey by Michael Henson, whose story "Probation" tackles the ravages of small town drug addiction and a woman trying to stay clean and sober; by emerging writer Rachel Garringer, who creates a strange and mystical world in "Not the Mountain Kind"; by Carter Sickels, author of the stunning novel *The Evening Hour*, whose essay chronicles his emerging identity as transgender and Appalachian; by bestselling novelist Denise Giardina in a scene from her first play *Robert and Ted*. You will pause to consider the words of poets like Rachel Morgan and Catherine Pritchard Childress, who write of absent family members and discovering what's right in front of you. And in this issue's craft essay, you will explore with novelist and memoirist Karen Salyer McElmurray the act of transforming experience into art, both fiction and creative nonfiction, and why memoir remains a relevant and thriving literary genre "in this often self-referential world."

But before you depart, please take time to applaud the winners of the 2013 Denny C. Plattner Awards, presented to the authors of the work deemed by our judges to be the best pieces of fiction, creative nonfiction, and poetry that appeared in the magazine last year.

The finest writing, Styron noted that day in Paris, should move the reader on multiple levels, "not only in its style, but in its total communicability, like the effect of good poetry." I guarantee that the writing in this issue will leave you moved—and slightly exhausted, but only in the best possible way. ■

2013 DENNY C. PLATTNER AWARDS

The annual Plattner Awards were established in 1995 by Kenneth and Elissa Plattner to honor their late son and his love of writing. The awards are given to the finest pieces of fiction, creative nonfiction, and poetry that appeared in *Appalachian Heritage* during the previous year. Winners receive a $200 prize and a handsome cherry wooden book rack designed and manufactured by Berea College Crafts.

FICTION

Judged by Glenn Taylor, author of The Marrowbone Marble Company *and* The Ballad of Trenchmouth Taggart

Winner: William Kelley Woolfitt, "Daughter with a Star on Her Brow"
Honorable Mention: Carrie Mullins, "Cell-Life"

CREATIVE NONFICTION

Judged by Marianne Worthington, author of Larger Bodies Than Mine *and co-editor of* Still: The Journal

Winner: Toby D. Gibson, "The Melungeons of Newman's Ridge: An Insider's Perspective"
Honorable Mention: Wendell Berry, "To Break the Silence"

POETRY

Judged by Irene Latham, author of The Sky Between Us *and* Leaving Gee's Bend

Winner: Stephanie Thomas Berry, "Guard the Night"
Honorable Mention: Samantha Cole, "Dreams of Family Buried in the Motor City"

PROBATION

MICHAEL HENSON

Maggie Boylan sat in her place and glared at the judge as hard a glare as she dared to give. But her glare was nothing to him. He kept his eyes on the papers laid out on the bench and he nodded as the lawyers—her lawyer on one side and the prosecutor on the other—said those things that lawyers say when they're deciding someone's case.

Finally, at a word from the judge, Maggie's lawyer nodded to the prosecutor and the prosecutor nodded to the judge and the judge wrote something on the papers and the little circle of men broke up.

Her lawyer sat back down beside her. He shrugged. "We got as good a deal as we're gonna get," he whispered.

She whispered back, "Did you get me off?"

"Maggie, I pulled out everything I had, but God himself couldn't have got you off this one."

"I didn't pay God to be my lawyer."

"If it comes to that, you didn't pay me either. The county pays my tab, for what it's worth."

"Well, what did the county get for its money?"

"The judge'll tell us in just a minute."

"Cooper, I swear I didn't do it."

"You can swear all you want. They had a witness."

"And that witness lied."

"But the judge believed her."

"I told you we should of gone for a jury trial."

"Maggie, there's not twelve people in this county you haven't pissed off."

"I ain't going back to prison."

"There's not twelve people in this county that haven't caught you in a lie."

"There's nothing on earth gonna make me go back to Marysville."

"I've caught you in a few lies myself."

"I'll hide out in the hills. I'll live off of squirrel meat and raw grass."

"Hush, Maggie." He tapped her arm and pointed to the bench.

"I'm telling you, I ain't going back to prison."

"Maggie, hush."

She would have given him a *hush-my-ass*, but the bucket-blue eye of the judge stared her into silence. He glared at her so hard she felt she had been nailed to the back of her seat.

The bailiff called out, "The defendant will now rise."

Cooper stood, but Maggie could not rise until the judge lowered his gaze and looked back down to his papers.

■■■

"Guilty as charged," the judge said. Three years on the shelf. Treatment in lieu of incarceration.

"If you fail to meet these obligations, if you are found in association with any known drug dealers or users, if you are found to be positive for alcohol or any other drug as evidenced by urinalysis or breathalyzer, if you pick up any new charge, if you get so much as a parking ticket, you will serve your full sentence with no hope of parole."

He set down the papers. "Do you understand me?"

"I got to go to a program?"

"And you will complete the program."

"I ain't going back to prison?"

"Not if you follow the rules of your probation."

Maggie cut her eye toward her lawyer. *Ain't he the smug one,* she thought.

The judge went on. "But if you fail to comply with these provisions, if you miss so much as a single meeting with your probation officer or with any counselor, therapist, or case manager recommended for you by your probation officer, I will see to it that you serve every minute of this suspended incarceration. Moreover, if you are caught so much as looking in the direction of a known user or seller of drugs, you will serve out the sentence that I have decided, this one time and against my better judgment, to suspend. Do you understand me?"

Maggie understood; she nodded her head to let him know she understood.

"For the record, Maggie, do you understand what I just told you?"

"Yes." She glanced toward Cooper. He nodded. "Yes, Your Honor," she said. "I do."

"So if I ever see you in this courtroom again during those three years or after, I will personally and promptly see to it that they put you under the jail."

■ ■ ■

"You'd have thought somebody would have been there for me," she told her husband over the phone. "But there wasn't a soul in that room there to back me up. There was Cooper, but he was paid to be there, you know what I mean? It's not the same. And he's just buddying up with those courthouse cronies and cutting deals instead of getting me off, cause, I know I done

She would have given him a hush-my-ass, but the bucket-blue eye of the judge stared her into silence.

a lot of things in my time, but this is one time I didn't do what they got me accused of. And I still got convicted. And now I'm on probation, they won't let me visit you in the jail no more. I'm just lucky they let me make this phone call. And they're talking about sending me to some treatment center in a whole another county, so I might as well be locked up."

"But, Maggie, it's ... "

"And I can't believe that motherfucking whore boldface lied on the stand like that. On the stand! Perjured her ass bigger'n life. I mean, don't they put people in jail for lying on the stand?"

"You ever done anything and not got caught?"

Maggie paused. She knew where this was going to go.

"I don't want to sound mean, but if you'd got what you deserved, you'd be wearing the orange jump suit and I'd be the one setting on the porch."

"But the bitch lied."

"And you never lied?"

"I never lied on the stand."

"Maggie ..."

"I always owned up to my shit."

"Maggie!" he said it sharp this time. "You know better and I know better and whoever's tapping this phone will know better if I have to spell it out."

She was quiet for a moment. "No," she said. "You don't need to spell it out."

A buzzer went off somewhere on her husband's end of the line. "I got to go now, Maggie. We'll talk tomorrow."

For a moment, Maggie couldn't speak.

"Maggie?"

"They'll still let you take my call?"

"They'll let us talk. Me and Irby go way back."

Maggie thought she should say something, but she could not find words.

"Do you hear me, Maggie? It's lights out. They're taking us back to the pod."

Maggie found her voice and said goodnight. She set the phone back on its cradle but she did not let it go. She sat and held onto the handset for several minutes before she finally reached around for her cigarettes. She tapped one out and lit it. She turned on the radio, just for the noise of it, and sat smoking with full attention. She smoked the cigarette down to the filter, stubbed it out fiercely, and reached for the phone again.

This time, she called her mother and asked to talk to the kids.

And yes, she knew it was a school night and yes, she knew it was late but no, her mother would not wake them at such an hour, and why did she call anyway at such an hour? What was she thinking? And yes, her mother knew she had gone to court but she had other things to do. And Maggie understood that but she swore she didn't do it and now she had to go to treatment and no, she didn't see how that could be a good thing when she didn't even do it. *And no, you don't understand; you never did understand. You just left me to fend for myself and now you won't even let a mother talk to her children. I don't care what hour it is and no, I'm not high but I might as well be for all the respect I get and all the good it does me to try and do right. Now don't hang up, no don't.*

But the line went dead on her mother's end.

This time, Maggie threw the phone down hard. It bounced off the cradle and clattered onto the floor.

■ ■ ■

It wouldn't be so bad, Maggie thought, *it if wasn't for the boys across the road up on Pillhead Hill.*

From early in the morning and late into the night, cars ran up Maggie's road from the south and down her road from the north. One by one, the tires of the cars wrestled with the turn, rattled the plank floor of the bridge over the creek, and barked up the gravel lane to the top of the hill.

All Maggie had to do was walk across the road and climb the hill and the boys at the top of the hill would take care of her. She had been up that hill and she knew that whatever she wanted—speed, Oxys, weed—the boys on the hill would have it. And if she had no money, they would front her, as any good neighbor would do.

But she could not relieve herself of the glare of the judge. All day long and late into the night, she felt the galvanized eye of the judge pierce her and fix her in place like a butterfly on a pin.

■ ■ ■

"So, Maggie," the probation officer said. "We meet again."

Her P.O. was a black-headed, black-bearded bear of a man whose elbows occupied most of a small wooden desk. He folded his big hands, hunched his shoulders, and loomed across the desk.

"We're right back where we started."

Maggie had been waiting in the hall outside his office for the better part of an hour; she was ready for a cigarette. "How long will this take?"

"How much time do you have?"

"Not much. I got to be somewhere."

"Well, Maggie. Right now, I think you're right where you need to be."

Maggie was not convinced of that, but she stayed in her seat. "All right," she said. "What do we have to do?"

There were papers to sign. Rules to review. "It's real simple," he said. "If you stay away from the alcohol and drugs, pay me a visit once a week, and stay out of trouble, then you get to stay out of jail."

"So why do I have to go to treatment?"

"Maggie, if you didn't need the treatment, you wouldn't even ask."

"But I've been clean for two months or more."

He thumbed through her file until he came to a lab report. "More like a month and a half."

"Whatever. I've stayed clean before for three and four months."

"And what happened?"

Maggie looked at her watch, realized she didn't have a watch, then looked around the room for a clock on the wall.

"Right, you got high again. You see," he said, "lots of people can stay clean for a good long while if they have something external, like the threat of prison, to keep them on track. But to make it last..."

"Okay, so what about...?"

He cut her off with a quick gesture. "To make it last," he said, "you have to learn to want it."

"And going to treatment is gonna make that happen?"

"If you let it happen."

"What about the known users and sellers part?"

"That too."

"How am I supposed to stay away from users and sellers

She had been up that hill and she knew that whatever she wanted—speed, Oxys, weed—the boys on the hill would have it.

when half the county is either using or selling or both, and everybody knows who's using and selling and nobody does a damn thing about it?"

"Do you know how porcupines make love?"

Here's another motherfucker pleased with himself, she thought. She sat as grim as she knew how and glared at him. "You know she lied, don't you?"

"Who lied?"

"That bitch that testified against me."

The P.O. looked around the room. "Is she in here?"

"Hell no, she ain't here."

"Then I don't see what she's got to do with what we're talking about."

"I wouldn't be here if it wasn't for her."

"Well, remind me to send her a thank you note."

"Thank you note for what?"

"See, you're on a track to be another statistic. But I'm convinced you can make it if you get the right help. She's your ticket to getting the help."

"She's a lying little crack whore is what she is."

"You know you never answered my question."

"What question?"

"How do porcupines make love?"

"What the hell do I know about a porcupine?"

"You know about those sharp quills. You know that if you get too close, you're liable to get stung."

"And..."

"So how do porcupines make love?"

"I don't know. Tell me."

"Very carefully."

"So what's your point?"

"Did you ever know a porcupine to hang around with a lying crack whore?"

"Of course not."

"That's one reason I've never had a porcupine in this office. They don't hang around with lying crack whores."

"Can I go now?"

"Be careful, Maggie. Be very careful who you hang out with. And don't go climbing up Pillhead Hill."

■ ■ ■

"So why," Maggie wanted to know, "do they have to pick on me when there's half a dozen meth labs right under their noses?"

“They offered you a chance to name some names and break down the charges,” her husband said from his end of the phone, “and you wouldn’t take it.”

“Which is why I’m still alive to tell you about it. And how did you hear that anyway?”

“Walls talk, babe.”

“Damn walls never talked to me when I was in the can.”

“It’s cause you never learned to listen.”

“I listen to you, don’t I?”

Her old man was silent for a moment.

Oh shit, she thought. *He’s gonna tell me something I don’t want to hear.*

“Maggie,” he said. He may have been set to tell her something she didn’t want to hear, but the buzzer sounded from his end of the line.

“It’s lights out, Maggie,” he said. “I got to go.”

■ ■ ■

A few days later, an old friend got Maggie a job waiting tables at the Square Deal Grill. Out the front window, if she stood right, she could see the jailhouse and the window where she thought her man might sometimes look out. Edie Pendarvis, her friend at the grill, was sober two years or more. She worked the same shift and picked Maggie up in the morning, brought her home in the afternoon, and took her to meetings three nights a week. Stavros, the owner, was nice to let her work, considering her record and all and knowing she would have to go for treatment as soon as a bed was open.

“You do right, Maggie,” he said in his Greek accent. “We’ll stand by you. You do right, you’ll always have a job here.”

He did not say what would happen if she did not do right. But she intended to do as right as she knew how. She had no intention of sitting under the steel-eyed glare of that judge again. She had no intention of taking that van back to Marysville.

Once or twice a week, the judge came in for lunch or for coffee and pie. Sometimes he nodded to her. Sometimes he spoke. Most times he ignored Maggie altogether—which was a blessing, for she could not look at the metal of his eye lest he pin her in place with a coffee pot in her hand.

Three weeks into the job with everything going well, that girl who lied put her head in the door. Things were slow after the breakfast run and Maggie had paused to stretch a newspaper over the counter. The only customer was a logger

The girl backed up. Her face went pale as bone. Her eyes went dark. Her right hand searched the pocket of her coat...

with wood chips in his hair sitting over coffee at the counter three stools down.

The girl paused at the door to speak to someone in the street, then started to walk toward the counter. She saw Maggie and stopped as if she had hit a wall.

"You lying bitch," Maggie whispered. *I'll kill her,* she thought. *I'll kill her right here.*

The girl backed up. Her face went pale as bone. Her eyes went dark. Her right hand searched the pocket of her coat; her left hand reached to find the door handle.

Maggie slapped the paper down. She would have pounced on the girl like a cat on a mole but for the counter in her way. By the time the girl found the door handle, Maggie was out from behind the counter, but Edie had her by the reins of her apron strings.

“I’ll kill her,” Maggie said. “I’ll kill her right there in the street.”

“No, you won’t,” Edie said. “I’ll kill you first.” She grabbed Maggie by the shoulder, pulled her back two steps, and moved in front to block Maggie from the door.

Maggie side-stepped. Edie stepped with her, then back when Maggie tried again. Satisfied that she had Maggie stopped for now, she stuck a bony finger like a pistol right between Maggie’s eyes. “Back up. Go straight back behind that counter,” she said. “Stay there and read your damn newspaper.”

■ ■ ■

And then one day there was Randy the Man.

“Here’s your neighbor,” Edie said. She touched Maggie at the elbow and pointed to the front booth. Randy the Man was the chief of the boys on the Pillhead Hill. He was tall and built like a bullet. He had eyes grey as lead and long grey hair cinched at the back of his neck. Blue tattoos too dense and obscure to read or interpret ran all up and down his arms and around his neck like the collar of a priest. He walked the square, broad step of a wrestler, which they said he had been—though not one of the famous ones—so when he strode into the Square Deal Grill, it was as if he were working his way through the crowd and up to the ring. It was as if he could hear the announcer call out, *here we have Randy the Man*.

“I can’t wait on him,” Maggie said.

“It’s your table,” Edie said.

“You don’t understand.”

“It’s your table.”

“You don’t fucking understand.”

“You told me you didn’t ever score from him.”

“I don’t. I mean, I don’t score from anybody now. But I never did. Or I did, but I couldn’t deal with the drama. It was

Dodge City up there, all them guns and hookers and young girls and I'm like..."

"He needs his coffee."

No one knew Randy the Man last summer when he first bought the old Stephens place across the creek and up the hill from Maggie's house. But they all knew him soon enough.

He paid cash up front, they said. And never blinked at the price. He just reached in his pocket and peeled off bills like cabbage leaves.

That got people's attention. But when he started selling Oxycontin off the front porch, his name was on every tongue.

Maggie got on the phone to her husband. "It can't last," she said. "There's too many people that know too much."

"Well, then stay away," he said.

But when he started selling Oxycontin off the front porch, his name was on every tongue.

"I don't want to be nowhere near that hill when it all goes to hell in a handbasket."

But the months turned around and the raid never came. Who was Randy paying off? Whose pocket was he lining? Or was he just that slick?

Night after night, cars ran down the road from the north or up the road from the south, cars in all states of operation, rumbling, rattling, or humming, to scrawl around the turn onto Randy's lane, rattle the bridge floor, and to mount the gravel lane to where Randy waited on the porch, ready to take the driver for that little walk back into the woods.

"I think he's up there committing slow suicide," Maggie told her old man. She had her own connections, so she stayed away, even after Randy told her, right on the courthouse square, "We got you covered," by which she understood that Randy the Man would front her if ever she came up dry.

And many a night, when she couldn't hook up, Maggie lay in a detoxified fever, burning and nauseous, crazy sick, her shocked cells demanding just a little hit, just a stupid little up front hit to take this pain away.

She shivered and cursed and hoped to die, but *I'm damned,* she thought, *if I'm going up that hill.*

But eventually, sometimes, she did. Terrible things happened, but sometimes she made that climb.

But that was over now. She was through with Pillhead Hill and anyone associated with it

"What if my P.O. sees me?"

"You ain't setting up housekeeping with him," Edie said.

"But ..."

"It's business. Take care of your business."

Maggie readied a cup and poured it full. She muttered a curse with as low a mutter as she knew how, but Edie said, "He'll want the whole pot, so you might as well bring it over. And I don't care what kind of bitches you call me."

Maggie took the cup in one hand and the pot in the other and muttered her way to Randy's booth. He let her set the coffee in front of him without taking his eye from the window. He waved away the cream and the sugar she tried to give him.

"You doing all right, Maggie?"

"I'm doing fine," she said. She couldn't look at him for fear of the judge, so she looked out the window as well. "Everything's fine," she mumbled.

"Your old man still over in the jailhouse?"

"Yeah, he's still in there."

"And he's got another couple months?"

That, she thought, *and another six days.* But she just nodded.

"I'm glad to see you working," Randy said. "I thought you were gone to Marysville for sure."

Maggie wanted to tell him all about the little lying crack whore and the judge with the galvanized eye, but she thought better of it. "I'm still here," she said.

"And I hear you're clean."

She wanted to ask, *Who told you that?* Instead, she let him tell her how good a thing that was and how she'll not regret it and how he wished he could quit smoking or for that matter this damn coffee which he drank five or ten pots of every day and it's the first thing in the morning and the last thing at night and he don't hardly get any sleep what with the coffee and those boys that's staying with him but hey, people gotta do what they gotta do, you know? *They sure like to party, but me, I like to...*

Randy seemed to have forgotten what he liked. Without another word, he set down his coffee, stood, slapped a five-dollar bill down on the table, and pushed past Maggie and out the door.

Randy seemed to have forgotten what he liked. Without another word, he set down his coffee, stood, slapped a five-dollar bill down on the table, and pushed past Maggie and out the door.

He balanced a moment on the front step of the Square Deal Grill. He gave a hard look to the main door of the courthouse, a brief look, a glance, but hard enough to drive a nail. Then he crossed the sidewalk in his squared-up wrestler's walk, opened the door of his Jeep, hammered down another glance toward the courthouse door, settled in behind the wheel, and drove off with his fat tires squealing.

A moment later, as if summoned by Randy's hard eye, Maggie's judge came out the courthouse door. Not the front door, but a little, hardly used, side door. He walked straight across the lawn to where the county reserved a spot for his SUV, got in, and drove off in the same direction as Randy the Man.

Maggie stared down the street until both cars took the bend in the road and disappeared. Then she set the pot back on the coffeemaker.

"You're not gonna believe this," she said.

"I never do," said Edie.

"No, really," Maggie said. "I just saw that judge that sentenced me take off after Randy the Man."

"And?"

"Why would that judge want to see Randy the Man?"

"He's a judge. He can see anybody he wants."

"Well, what's he gonna do with Randy the Man?"

"He's a judge. He can do what he wants."

"But what if he's buying drugs?"

"He's a judge."

"But don't he have to follow the law like the rest of us?"

"How many judges did you know up in Marysville?"

"Not a one."

"There's my point."

"What point?"

"He's a judge. He's got the law in his hip pocket."

"But that ain't right."

"Maggie, what do you know about right? You been wrong since you first drew breath and now you want to talk about right?"

Why, Maggie wondered, *is everybody so dedicated to setting me straight?*

"You don't know any more than a bird about what that judge is up to. You don't even know for sure he was following Randy."

"I seen him."

"You just happened to see him get in a car right after Randy the Man got in a car and you just happened to see him drive for a few blocks that just happened to be in the same direction as Randy the Man. And you think you can make a case from that?"

I saw what I saw, thought Maggie. *I saw what I saw.*

■■■

One after another, day and night, the cars came down Maggie's road from the north and up her road from the south. They worked through the turn, shook the bridge floor, scratched their way up the hill and, minutes later, rolled back down. Sometimes, a bright, new SUV scrambled up the hill and an old beater rolled back down, and Maggie knew that someone had gotten the bad end of a deal and their car would end up in the row of cars parked behind the house. And one day she thought she knew the SUV that went up the hill and thought she saw her judge driving the beater that came back.

This ain't right, she thought. But she said nothing at the Grill and nothing on the phone to her old man.

And the boys on the Pillhead Hill continued night and day. Sometimes, when the wind was right, Maggie heard snatches of music way up into the night, or high-pitched women's laughter, or the gunning of a motorcycle that set the dogs to barking all up and down the road.

As the cars came from north and south, each one bore a bank account, a week's pay, or fifty dollars from selling off the piano someone's grandmother left them. They carried the college tuition, the Christmas toys for the kids, the house payment, the support payment, the car payment that was overdue. They carried the egg money or tobacco money or money earned giving blowjobs to truckers. Entire houses went up the hill, along with farms and small businesses, reputations, and self-respect. Years went uphill, bundled like cordwood, stacked for sale, ready to burn.

It's a terrible thing that happens up there on that hill, Maggie thought. But she longed for the terrible thing. Each frailed and fouled nerve was alert to the chance. Each addled neuron ached to be filled with that ecstasy and disaster.

She only wanted a reason.

■ ■ ■

She was in the habit of calling Gary the last thing at night before he had lights out and before she had to try to sleep before work. But this time when she called, it wasn't Irby, the usual second-shift jailer.

"Who's this?" she asked.

"Deputy Weatherstone."

"Timmy?"

"Who's this?"

"Timmy, let me talk to Gary real quick before it's lights out."

"Can't do it, Maggie."

"Why not? I call every night."

"I got orders, Maggie."

He had orders. She argued, but Timmy Weatherstone had orders, in writing, in plain sight, and he didn't care what Irby did on his shift and he wasn't going to let her talk to him like that and how did she get this number anyway? She cursed him seven times blue and reminded him what a snake he had for a mother before he hung up on her with a curse of his own and she thought, *Now I've gone and done it.* She was gospel sure she was headed off to Marysville on the next bus north.

So why not?

■ ■ ■

This is just like death, Maggie thought. She was warm, she was at peace, she was free of pain. Everything was still. She was swaddled in light.

She tested her limbs and found that her arms and legs were heavy as timber.

This is what death is like, she thought. *This might be death itself.*

But death would not perch an IV bottle over her like a plastic buzzard. Death would not run a tube down into her arm and death would not post a monitor with red blinking lights by her bedside. She propped herself up and widened her gaze. Death, she knew, was not a hospital room and death would not leave so bearish a man asleep in a chair nearby.

She thought she knew him, but she did not know the big yellow teeth exposed by the man's slack jaw. Perhaps he sensed that someone was staring at him, for he caught himself mid-snore, pulled his lips down over the teeth, and looked around. When he saw it was Maggie, he brightened.

"So you're back among the living."

"What're you doing here?"

"I've been taking a little power nap," he said. "The real question is what are you doing here?"

Maggie looked around and shrugged. "I don't even know how I got here."

"You know you just about took the big nap."

She shrugged, as if to say she would not have minded. "So I reckon I'll be going back to prison."

"Maggie," he said. "If you can't be careful you might as well be lucky. And you're a lucky woman. You're lucky to be alive and you're lucky enough to time your overdose for a Friday night just before a treatment bed came open."

"So what does that mean?"

"It means that if I can get you out of here and into that treatment bed before court opens on Monday, you don't go back to prison."

"What day is it now?"

"It's Sunday evening; we've got to be rolling."

Within an hour, Maggie was pronounced fit to leave. A nurse untethered her from the IV and the monitor, stood her up on her shaky feet, helped her dress, and rolled her in a wheelchair to the parking lot where her P.O. waited in his car.

It was growing dark and snow had begun to fall as they pulled out of the lot.

"Can I go home first?"

"We're not taking any chances." He took one big paw off the steering wheel and pointed to the back seat with his thumb. "Your girlfriend from the Grill packed a duffel for you. No need to risk starting this whole thing over."

Maggie fretted in her seat. "The meds is starting to wear off," she said. "I'm gonna start geeking soon."

"We'll get you there soon enough. And they'll give you whatever you need."

Maggie was not convinced, but there was nothing she could do about it. The treatment people, she knew, would just tell her to tough it out, though she did not feel tough at all, just now. She slumped in her seat and watched the lights of the houses roll by. Here and there, she caught a glimpse into a kitchen or a living room—a couple at table or the flicker of a television—and felt lonely and out of sorts.

What a mess my life has been, she thought.

They left town and the fields began to open up around them; the lights were fewer than before. They hit the highway and the car picked up speed. Her P.O., who had been silent and wary as they drove through town, began to talk about this and that. She supposed that she should listen. But mile after mile, she continued to watch the lights tick by, the lights of the houses near the road and the lights far out in the hills that, in their distance, might as well have been stars. ■

HOTEL
FEDERAL

LEGACIES

erased from Allen Tate's "Remarks on the Southern Religion"

the modern southerner inherits
a kind of history

he would like to believe
a vast hope   some magic

to spirit back to him
his way of life

he   in short   inherits
violence

R.C. NEIGHBORS

BATTLEFIELD

Mid-October, and around the rocks of Devil's Den
legions of cabbage white butterflies march
in wild disorder, like scattered clouds of ashes
in the late-day light. Under the blank staring eyes
of bronze generals we negotiate winding
dirt paths among boulders encrusted with shapeless
patches like grey-green lace: when I visited
Gettysburg as a child with my parents, I imagined
those splotches on the rocks to be long-weathered
remnants of spattered blood. I know now
they're lichens, fungi and algae interdependent,
forming a perfect union, and the real remains
of those three savage, scorching days
twelve-pound cannons belching thunder
mortar shells whistling and exploding
men and horses down, the wounded
crawling screaming cursing
are less obvious. At the outskirts of that regiment
of massive stones, a line of golden foxtails nods
in the breeze; a mockingbird whistles its contorted song,
mosquitoes whine past our ears. On the hillside
near Little Round Top withered stems of Solomon's
seal bearing shreds of twisted, frost-bleached
leaves lie flattened on the ground, their red fruits
spilling like tears down the grassy bank,
deepening shadows assembling around them
in pools of blue and grey.

CAROL GRAMETBAUER

JOHNSON CITY

CARTER SICKELS

Stephen was singing along and tapping his hands on the steering wheel to the Mountain Goats, one of his favorite bands. It was a good day for driving and singing. October blue sky, hills layered with oaks and maples and sweetgums flashing scarlet and gold leaves. We'd left Chapel Hill in the afternoon and were on our way to Johnson City, Tennessee, where Stephen was born and raised.

"Remember, don't call me Stephen around my granny," he said.

"What about around your parents?"

"Yeah. They won't but you should call me Stephen."

He reached to adjust his glasses, and then rubbed his finger over the naked patch of skin in front of his ear. This morning he had shaved off his sideburns and stubble, but there was nothing he could do about his deep voice.

"I don't get it. How can your granny not know?"

Stephen had started taking testosterone about eight months ago. He'd come out as transgender to his parents, but was too scared to tell his eighty-one-year-old grandmother, the woman who'd helped raise him. They'd seen each other many times since Stephen started physically transitioning, and his grandmother never asked questions. As long as she didn't say anything, Stephen wasn't going to either.

"I guess people see what they want to see," he said.

Stephen and I had met that summer. He was my closest friend in Chapel Hill, where we were both grad students at UNC. I'd moved there from New York. When I left the city, I was afraid I wouldn't find a queer community—I never dreamed that one of the first people I would meet would be a trans guy from East Tennessee.

Stephen pulled in to a gas station and parked his Subaru wagon behind a massive pickup. I followed him in the rundown store, feeling uneasy. Sometimes that's how it is when you walk into a straight space, especially in rural America—you know you don't belong, and they know it too.

But we were trying. We were wearing flannels and jeans and boots. Stephen read easily as male, even with the smooth face. He was tall, that helped, and his salt and pepper hair, neatly clipped, made him look older than thirty. Plus he had the low voice, the thick neck and strong jaw. Back then, I never knew how people were reading me. I was skinny and tall. I wore my hair short with a line of bangs angled toward my eyes. This was before I'd changed my name or started using male pronouns, and a long time before I even considered taking testosterone. Still, I didn't look the way a female is supposed to look. Mostly, I just confused people.

The grizzled guy behind the counter, sporting an impressive set of chops, wore a trucker hat with a deer patch on the front, a hat for which hipsters would pay good money. He watched us walk in, arms crossed over his chest.

"How you doing, buddy?" Stephen said.

Stephen's loose way with strangers, even with the straight, potentially scary kind, always eased the tension.

"All right, man, how are you?"

"Good. Real good."

While Stephen went to the men's room, I wandered the aisles, pretending to study rows of chips and candy, wondering what this guy thought of me. There were times I got called ma'am by one person then sir by the next in the span of about thirty seconds.

When Stephen came back out, he nodded at the guy. "Thank you, sir."

"Y'all have a good one."

Back on the road, I asked Stephen what he thought—how did that guy see me?

"He probably saw us as two guys," he said.

I didn't believe him, but it was nice to hear. I didn't know what I wanted exactly, except that I was feeling more and more uncomfortable being seen as a girl. I flinched whenever I heard the word "ma'am"—it came at me like a fist. But when someone called me "he," I opened up, swallowed the word, held it inside me.

"The way you were talking to that guy, it's so easy for you," I said.

"What do you mean?"

"You talked to him just like, like, this dude."

"That's just how I am. I would have acted the same way before." Stephen lit a cigarette, cracked the window. "I get nervous, too. Afraid someone will figure me out."

"What was the men's bathroom like?"

"Disgusting."

"Does it feel weird, you know, to go in there?"

"Sometimes."

"Did you use the men's bathroom before you started passing?"

"On and off. It depended."

"Makes me nervous," I said.

"The thing is, men don't notice shit," Stephen said. "Women will stare at you, they'll pay attention. But if you've got short hair and use the men's room, nobody will even look at you."

Stephen was used to my questions, used to me studying him. I intended to write my thesis on the trans community. I'd brought my camera and recorder to document our trip. I didn't call myself

I flinched whenever I heard the word "ma'am"—it came at me like a fist. But when someone called me "he," I opened up, swallowed the word, held it inside me.

transgender, not yet, but I was drawn to the stories in ways that I still couldn't articulate for myself, even though, to others, it must have been obvious how thirsty I was for recognition and validation.

We passed a boarded up farmhouse, a yard buried under gutted cars, a billboard that said *The only Path to God is to the Right,* and a yellow school bus, probably someone's home, parked in the middle of a pasture. The landscape reminded me of southern Ohio, where most of my family was from, where I used to visit my grandparents. The politics of these places scared the hell out of me, but there was something about them, with their old-time look and rundown beauty, that spoke to me—I wanted to touch the knotholes in the fences, smell freshly mowed hay, walk across fields. When I was living in New York, I'd gone away for six weeks to work on my novel in a cabin in Tennessee. Every morning I woke with the birds, then brewed coffee and wrote. No city noise to battle with, no high rent to worry over. With my life slowed down, I had more time to examine it. The truth was, I wasn't happy in New York. It was then that I started thinking about leaving, but it took me another two years to finally go.

Stephen turned onto a residential street and eased up on the gas. "We're here."

His parents lived in a neighborhood where most of the houses had been built in the sixties and seventies. Huge maples and oaks canopied the sidewalks and the spacious front yards, shedding fall leaves. Their house was a brick ranch with well-tended flowers curving along the walkway.

His parents came out through the garage to greet us. They were friendly and gracious, shook my hand and welcomed me, but their main focus was Stephen, their only child. His father patted him on the back. He was shorter than Stephen, with a rounder build. They both had the same bright blue eyes, both wore glasses.

When Stephen and his mother hugged, they rocked their bodies together. They had the same plum cheeks, big smiles.

"Supper's ready," his mother said. "And I made cupcakes for dessert."

"Oh good. Mama made cupcakes," Stephen said, smiling like a little kid.

His mother put the food out on the table: mashed potatoes, meatloaf, an iceberg lettuce salad, and green bean casserole that she probably made just for me, the vegetarian. She was worried I didn't have enough to eat and dished more on my plate. She and

Stephen did most of the talking. I liked listening. They drew out their vowels and said things like "I reckon" and "I was tickled," reminding me of home.

"Granny doesn't know I'm coming, does she?" Stephen asked his mother.

"No, I didn't tell her. She's going to be so happy to see you."

His parents also did not want Stephen to come out to his grandmother. Nobody thought she would be able to emotionally or physically handle it. "I just wouldn't have any idea how to tell her," Stephen said to me. "Not in a way that she'd ever understand. I can't imagine that she could fathom why on earth someone would want to change their 'God given' gender."

After supper, while Stephen's father watched TV, we looked at family pictures. Relatives, ancestors, stern men and women in dark clothes. And pictures of Stephen. In one of them, he wore a bunny costume for a dance class: a black leotard and silky pink bunny ears, long hair pulled in a ponytail.

"Mama," Stephen said. "That's embarrassing."

"She loved dance class," his mother told me. "And she played the fiddle too. We should show one of those videos of you playing the fiddle."

Stephen shot me a look when his mother used the wrong pronoun, but he didn't correct her. All evening, his parents kept calling him by his birth name and referring to him as "she" or "her." Sometimes Stephen didn't react, at least not outwardly; other times, his brow creased, his jaw clenched like he was biting down on all the pain he'd been carrying around for so long. To ease the hurt, I made sure to say his name a few times, to use male pronouns. Whenever I did, his mother just kept talking, her hands locked together in her lap like she was trying to hold herself together. She laughed a lot, but there was something sad in her expression, a wistfulness. Here was her thirty-year-old child, once her daughter, now a man.

Stephen told me that he and his mother used to fight a lot when he was in high school, especially after he came out as gay. Back then, still identifying as female, gay seemed like the only way to describe himself. His parents, both Democrats, were liberal up to a point, but still, his mother didn't approve. After she found a love letter that Stephen had written to a girl, she kicked him out. His father wasn't as upset: "I guess it's like being a Republican," he'd said. "I don't understand it, but it's your decision."

When Stephen came out as trans at twenty-nine, his mother cried. She also said, "I love you." She said, "You're my child." His parents were trying. They had given him a bouquet of flowers after his chest surgery, and his father had bought him a men's suit for a job interview. They would get better about using his name and the right pronoun, and Stephen would get better about correcting them. He wanted them to know who he was, he wanted to be seen.

■ ■ ■

For years I'd been living in this kind of unacknowledged space between female and male. I identified as female back then because I didn't see another option, not for myself. I felt like I wasn't allowed to have a trans story. That was for people who'd known all their lives, who felt like they'd been born in the wrong body. Those were the only stories I'd heard about trans guys. They lived as masculine females before medically transitioning. They worked on cars, played football. For them, I thought, their identity was a hard, clear light. For me, everything was cloudy, shadowy, shifting. I knew, and yet I didn't.

Then Stephen told me, "I never felt trapped in the wrong body. Some guys have that experience, but a lot of others don't." He added, "I also don't have early memories of, 'I'm a boy.'

"How did you know?" I asked, desperate for a bright, clanging sign. I was sick of the questioning and searching, the ambiguity.

"It's an ongoing process." Stephen saw gender as fluid, always changing. "I feel more comfortable presenting as male, you know, more comfortable in the world."

When I was living in New York, I caught glimpses of different kinds of transgender expressions and identities, but I didn't look too closely. If I did, I buried whatever I saw and convinced myself everything was fine, even when I stared at myself for too long in the mirror, worrying I looked too much like a girl. I resigned myself to admiring from afar chiseled jaws and flat chests, and I never spoke about transitioning. I didn't know how to change something so big, so connected to my identity, not until I moved to North Carolina, where I met Stephen and other trans people. Living in a quieter, slower, smaller place, I couldn't hide from myself as easily, and

They would get better about using his name and the right pronoun, and Stephen would get better about correcting them. He wanted them to know who he was, he wanted to be seen.

the dull pain that had been pressing down on me for so long slowly started to lift.

Stephen opened a door that I already knew was there, but I'd never looked to see what was behind it. Now, with the door open, I bombarded him with questions. How did it feel to change his name? To go swimming without a shirt? To be seen as a gay man around straight men? These were all things

I thought I'd never get to experience. "My parents would never understand," I told him.

"That's what I thought about mine, too," he said.

Many of my queer friends, rejected and hurt by their blood families, rarely spent time with them. Stephen was different; he was close to his family, and I liked that. I visited my parents several times a year, and, always happy to see each other, we held up our ends of an unspoken agreement to ignore what could be painful or scary. After so many years of silence, I didn't know how to suddenly start talking. Stephen understood. He told me, "We don't talk about anything difficult in my family. I certainly am not going to change that by coming out to my Granny."

My parents were getting old, and I didn't want to hurt them. If I ever transitioned, I thought, I would have to disappear.

In the morning, Stephen and I went to pick up his grandmother to take her back to his parents' house for brunch. Both of us were still waking up—Stephen with a big cup of sweet tea, me with coffee. His grandmother lived on the other side of town, about a fifteen minute drive from his parents'. The white house with rose-colored shutters sat on a corner of two quiet streets. She had been living there alone since her second husband, the only granddaddy that Stephen knew, died twenty-five years ago. Curtains and drapes blocked all the windows.

"You sure she's up?"

"She just doesn't like people looking in." Stephen raised his eyebrows, made his voice high like Granny's: "You can never be too careful."

Stephen rang the bell. His grandmother was expecting Stephen's father. After a few minutes, we heard footsteps, a fussing with the locks.

"Hold on," she called.

The door opened a crack, then wider.

Granny's wrinkled face broke into a smile that showed all her yellowing teeth. "My Lord," she said. "What in the world are you doing here?"

Laughing, Granny pulled Stephen to her. When he was a kid, he spent more time here than at his parents'. He stood a head taller than her. Her old, knobby, bent fingers pressed into the middle of his back like they were a part of his spine.

"Surprised?" Stephen asked.

"Well, no. I had a feeling," she said, gazing at him like he hadn't changed a bit.

The three of us stood in the entry way to the house on a little plastic runner that protected the ivory carpeting from dirt, Granny looking at Stephen like she couldn't tear her eyes away. I wondered what she saw. I'd expected him to wear layers, to hide in his clothes, maybe a baggy sweatshirt, but he had on a flannel that drew tight against his flat chest.

Granny didn't want to look away from her grandchild, but she was also curious about the stranger in her house.

"Hi, honey," she said to me, her voice warm and throaty, a smoker's voice, except that she'd never smoked. Granny grew up Methodist, then converted to Baptist. Stephen said she wasn't religious in a scary way though. "She's just very spiritual," he explained.

Granny fit her bony hand in mine. Her skin was tissue soft the way old people's often is. All my grandparents were dead, and I missed them. "It's so good to meet you," she said in a strong mountain lilt.

Next to Stephen, Granny seemed small, but she was not a tiny woman. If she could have stood straight, she would have been around 5'6". But her back was hunched, which made her head stretch out like a turtle's. She had a long, pretty face with prominent cheekbones and a strong jaw, a face that turned heads in her day.

"You from North Carolina?"

"Ohio," I said.

She asked if I knew the Beasleys. I said I didn't. She asked what my grandparents' last names were, where they had lived. She wanted to know who my people were.

"Granny, you can find all that out later," Stephen said. "You ready?"

"Not yet. I'm having a hard time getting around." Granny's smile fell. "Look here. Did your mom tell you I broke my toes?"

"How did you manage to do one on each foot?"

"Who knows. These things are slowing me down." Granny pointed to the bulky orthopedic sandals on her feet. "And look at how ugly."

"They're not so bad."

"Oh, yes, they are." Granny was dressed in black slacks and a lavender blouse, and I had the feeling she was the kind of lady who never wore sneakers or jeans.

Stephen tried to lighten the situation. "You like my shoes?"

We glanced at his worn out blue Nikes. "No, I don't like them." His grandmother also didn't like his hair. "I don't know why you have to wear it so short."

Stephen told her we had to go, his mother had lunch waiting.

"I've got to fix my face first," she said. "You two come on in here, keep me company."

In the hallway, I stopped to look at the framed photographs covering nearly every inch of the wall. Pictures of Stephen, relatives, friends. Family shots probably taken for church directories or Christmas cards: husband in a suit, wife in a dress, a couple of kids with their hair combed and faces scrubbed. One family looked vaguely familiar.

"Is that—" I looked at Stephen. He was laughing. "Does she know the Gores?"

"Not personally, but she's a big fan of Al's."

The photograph was from the nineties. The daughters and Tipper were smiling, and Al looked fresh-faced and presidential.

"The Clintons are up there too," Stephen said.

Right above a photograph of Stephen and his parents was one of Bill, Hillary, and Chelsea. I also saw Jimmy Carter and his family.

"She'll put a picture of the Obamas up there too," Stephen said. "She stayed up all night watching the election, she was so excited."

While Stephen and I sat on the edge of Granny's neatly made bed, she fluffed her white hair, sprayed her neck with heady perfume. I imagined Stephen had spent a lot of time in here watching her fix her face, and wondered if anything about the room had changed over the years. Angel figurines, in pastel pinks and lilacs, sat on a dainty shelf. A bouquet of red silk carnations. Bottles of pills, a box of tissues. Lacy white curtains in the windows like giant wings. Stephen was her only grandchild, and there were pictures of him everywhere. Baby pictures, school pictures. Same blue eyes, same smile. One of him with his honey-brown hair falling to his shoulders, folded hand propped under his chin. In another picture, maybe age four or five, he had pretty pink bows in his hair.

"I was prissy," Stephen told me. "I had some lovely bows."

I asked if I could take some photographs.

"Go ahead, she won't care."

Granny was too busy applying dark, respectable lipstick. She fussed with a brooch but her fingers were too bent, so Stephen pinned it to her blouse. He was gentle and careful with her. He helped her pick out a sweater, which took awhile, since everything he pulled from the closet Granny didn't like.

After she settled on a cardigan, she had to choose a scarf. She wrapped a green chiffon one around her neck. "You like this one or the purple one better?"

"The purple one," Stephen said.

She looked doubtful. "Maybe." Then she noticed my camera. I'd already taken some shots of her and Stephen. "Can you make our picture?" she asked.

Stephen leaned down so his face was even with his grandmother's and both of them smiled, old and young faces, female and male. Stephen had told me that he never thought he would be able to transition while his grandmother was still alive. "But then, I don't know, I just couldn't take it anymore," he said.

For as long as Stephen could remember, his grandmother had called him "my little girl." I wondered what she thought when she looked at him now. She wasn't stupid. Politically, she was fairly progressive. But Stephen said she wouldn't get it. "She operates in an incredibly gendered world," he said. "I don't know that she has a concept that transgender people exist."

Maybe he was right. Granny just didn't have the capacity to grasp the changes in her grandchild. Or maybe she thought if she continued to see Stephen as her granddaughter, her pride and joy, her "little girl," then this could be the only truth.

I never figured out what Stephen's grandmother did or didn't realize, or, if he had told her, if she would have accepted him. But I understood why Stephen chose not to—I felt similarly about my own parents.

"I don't want to disappoint her. I spend a lot of time trying to make my family happy," he said. "I don't want to make my Granny sad. I think that's my biggest fear."

Before we left, Granny made sure she had everything she needed in her pocketbook: house keys, lipstick, compact, blush, and a plastic light the size of an oatmeal cookie that turned on when you tapped it. It was something you might stick to a closet wall, but she carried it with her for emergencies.

She double and triple-checked the front door, making sure it was locked.

“You can’t be too careful. There are break-ins around here,” she said. “I get scared to death just going to town.”

“Scared of what?”

“Shoot-em-ups,” she said.

Stephen and I laughed, but she didn’t think it was funny. The world was a dangerous place, and nothing was the way it used to be.

Walking to the car, Granny suddenly stopped. She looked at me, then at Stephen. Her blue eyes were alert. For a second, I thought she was going to say something big, tell him she knew the truth and that it was okay. Her face lifted into a beaming smile.

“I’m just so glad you girls are here,” she said.

That word, how it snapped in the air, knocked us off balance, how it hurt. Stephen and I looking at each other over the top of Granny’s head, we held each other’s gaze, something like laughter but stranger and darker and sadder rising between us. We were together in this surreal, alternate universe. What did she see when she looked at me, when she looked at him, that allowed the word “girls” to make sense?

“Come on, Granny.” Stephen tried to make things normal again. “Mama’s probably wondering what in the world happened to us.”

■ ■ ■

“Want a beer?” Stephen yelled over the thumping music.

We were at New Beginnings, the only gay bar in East Tennessee. This was the breath of fresh air, smoky as it was, that we needed. It had been a long day of eating too much, looking at family pictures, pretending. Stephen getting called by his birth name. Me not knowing who I was or wanted to be.

He handed me a PBR and we crossed a wide open dance floor. There was a stage and catwalk, and a separate room with pool tables and a TV. The over-the-top decorating styles competed with each other: zebra print chairs, ancient Greek-style pillars and arches, strobe lighting. There was also a gift shop that sold T-shirts and sex toys.

The crowd was mostly men. That's also why Stephen and I were there—to feel a part of something that for so long had been out of reach. Both of us had spent significant years identifying as lesbians, but, like Stephen said, "It just never felt totally right." Being with women, identifying as women, had made some kind of sense at the time, but not anymore. Tonight we wanted to explore this part of ourselves that felt truer. We were wearing tight jeans and snap-buttoned plaid cowboy shirts, like the kind my grandfather used to wear. Every so often a guy met my eyes, but I looked away, not sure if I was passing or not. I stood close to Stephen, my bodyguard.

A black drag queen in a shimmering slinky blue dress belted out "The Greatest Love of All," and a straight-looking white guy in front of me, skinny with a buzz-cut and Marines T-shirt, wolf whistled. Others slipped dollar bills in Whitney's cleavage. If only Granny could see this. It wasn't like the drag shows in New York or Portland or San Francisco. This was all about realness. No social satire, no comedy or shock, no bearded guys in women's bathing suits. This was old-school, all Patti Labelle, Cher, Diana Ross. Teased wigs, sparking lipstick, sequined gowns. Some of the performers' timing was way off, and one queen didn't know even half the words, but they never lost the crowd's attention or adoration. They danced and twirled and pranced up and down the catwalk in platform heels and thigh high boots, beautiful spectacles of femininity.

While Stephen went to the bathroom, I waited at the bar, checking out guys in the mirror behind the bottles of liquor, all these pretty pieces of glass I was afraid to touch. One day, not long after we'd met, Stephen had studied me and said he didn't know how I'd ever called myself butch. "You're too prissy, too gay," he said. "A gay guy, I mean." What he said struck a deep chord of recognition within me, but I was still too scared and wracked by self-doubt, and I just laughed him off.

There were a few cowboy types, but most guys were wearing tight T-shirts or tank tops, their hair clipped short. High-pitched laughter, exclamations of "Girl, please," made me smile. A tall older man standing next to me gazed at my reflection in the mirror, and I looked down at my beer, my heart racing.

Then Stephen was next to me, his cheeks flushed. "Some guy just kissed me."

"What? Who? When?"

They danced and twirled and pranced up and down the catwalk in platform heels and thigh high boots, beautiful spectacles of femininity.

"Just now, when I was in the bathroom. There was only one stall and the damn door didn't lock, and then this guy pushed open the door."

"He see anything?"

"No. I started to walk out and he said, 'You're cute.' And then he grabbed me and started kissing me." Stephen's words came out fast, a teenager talking about a crush. I kept forgetting that he was still new to this world too, still finding his way.

"Dude, that's awesome. You're in."

Stephen passed in ways that I couldn't, not yet. Passing isn't the right word: this was just who he was. And what I felt when I looked at him was the ache to touch that kind of truth in myself.

■ ■ ■

Stephen and I were leaving East Tennessee and heading back to North Carolina. We passed empty fields and forests that popped with color. Spirals of smoke rose up from the occasional farmhouse, a sight that made us nostalgic for a way of life we'd never lived. For Stephen, his Appalachian roots were a solid part of his identity. I couldn't exactly claim this, but my memories of spending time at my grandparents,' the pull I felt toward the language and place, made me feel connected to something bigger than myself.

"You think my granny knows something?"

He was looking straight ahead. We were the only car on the road.

"I don't know. It seems like you've figured out a way to be yourself around her."

"That's the thing, I'm not."

We drove in silence for awhile, then Stephen pointed out a log cabin on a hill, craggy mountains rising behind it. "I'd like to live there," he said.

The place looked just about perfect, and for an instant, I felt the same desire: to wake up every day with a view of the forest and mountains, to grow vegetables and chop wood and read by the light of the fire.

"Don't you think it would be hard to live here? Especially if you had a partner."

"Not if I had a girlfriend," he said.

"What if you had a boyfriend?"

Stephen rubbed his chin where the short hairs were growing back. "That's a different story. No, I couldn't live here if I was with a boy."

"We'd get killed."

"We? Yeah, I reckon we might." He glanced at me. "You sure know how to bring a person down."

The road followed a river that snaked in and out of the forest. Stephen shifted into a lower gear. For awhile, we were quiet. I wanted to apologize, but I didn't know why.

"I miss being able to go to family things," he said. "All my mom's side of the family lives in Virginia, and we used to have these big Thanksgivings. I can't do that now because everyone will know." He paused. "I miss seeing the old people in my family."

Stephen came to a place where there was room to pull over and turned off the engine. My chest ached like I was binding, all these secrets, the exhaustion of trying to protect my parents, to hide myself, everything so tightly wound and hidden. Transitioning isn't just about change, it's also about loss, letting go.

"My parents, it would kill them. I'd never get to see them again," I said. I didn't want to disappoint them. I didn't want to make them sad.

The engine was ticking like the sound in my chest. Stephen looked at me with soft eyes. "You don't know that."

"I've wanted to change my name for years," I said. "I never thought I could. What if it's too late?"

"It's not too late," Stephen said. "It's never too late."

Stephen already saw me as a boy, he saw my true gender. But it went deeper than that. He saw me for who I was. He put his hand on my knee. There isn't just one trans story in the world, Stephen taught me that. There isn't just one way to be.

"One day you might surprise yourself, how you decide to be around your parents. Hell, they might surprise you too."

His hand was still on my knee, the fingers curled, waiting. The tightness in my chest began to fade, and I turned toward him, our faces so close. He could see what I couldn't yet.

"Come on," he said.

We got out and crossed the road, twigs and acorns crunching under our shoes. Here we had an open and up close view of the river and a small waterfall. The day was clear, and a hard light gave everything an extra shine. Yellow hickory leaves, the black bark of the oaks. River rushing over boulders. Leaves decaying into the ground, returning to where they came from.

"I feel completely different when I'm in the mountains," Stephen said. "It's just different. It just feels different."

I knew what he meant. We felt more at home here than we ever would be at a gay bar or around our families. Here, there was nothing to explain. Stephen somehow was making it work; maybe I could too, maybe I wouldn't have to disappear—instead, maybe I would finally be seen. We stood next to each other as ourselves, surrounded by forest that was millions of years old and feeling content with all its mystery. Here, now, the two of us, we could just be. ■

What'll You Have?
Pabst Blue Ribbon
Now Serving
PBR 24oz. Cans
$3.50
CASH

HOTEL ISLAND

Young lungs strain
against the stricture
of the life jacket.
Ahead my father's shoulders
bob like a long-tailed
duck riding, then diving
into a ripple. He is young.
Between breaths, we compare
what we may find
on the island. My sister
wants to find a hoopskirt
a real Victorian lady
wore to a ball. She is
a romantic. I want to find
broken wineglasses, because
I've never seen wine or a glass
designed to hold it.
Colleen wants to find a body.

The shell covering the beach
is dangerous as broken plates.
Lake water dries sticky on our skin.

Ahead, my father hops,
yelping like a coyote,
at pretend discoveries.
We believe he sees the ghosts
of vacationers. He hoists
an ochre shell shaped
like a pistol's grip.

We never found what
we imagined we would.
The way back is always shorter
because anticipation takes hope.

Between strokes his arms
reach ferris wheel high.
He says TVA flooded the valley
below our scissor-kicking feet.
Cows ran for high ground;
farmers lugged suitcases
of try-hard and tough luck.
The hotel's fine china a parable
for the derelict and dreamful.

RACHEL MORGAN

COLONY COLLAPSE DISASTER

The venom, he believed, was good for the heart.
Like some strange astronaut crossing the yard,
he confessed to the bees: the happiness of his
marriage, enabling his son's alcoholism, the man
he shot in World War II, the almanac's weather.

The cause never matters, but the absence does:
snaggle-toothed children on post office posters,
Bermuda Triangle boats and planes, an aging woman's
hope to conceive, whole colonies of bees can vanish.

As a child Everette was taught to sprinkle
bees with flour and then follow the ghost trail
to the hive. Now would the path stop mid-field?

It wasn't exactly his heart, but the anti-arrhythmia drugs
that drowned the hive of his lungs. Two years after,
I open the last jar of honey my grandfather put up.
A sweetness that aches astounds me. Papery bits of comb
stick to my teeth like what I still can't speak of.

RACHEL MORGAN

ROBERT AND TED

An excerpt from the play

DENISE GIARDINA

For thirty years, Denise Giardina has captivated readers with nationally bestselling novels including *Storming Heaven, Saints and Villains, Good King Harry,* and *Emily's Ghost.* But more recently, the acclaimed novelist has turned to the stage, writing a powerful two-act play titled *Robert and Ted,* which traces the relationship between the late Senators Robert Byrd of West Virginia and Edward M. Kennedy of Massachusetts.

With an historian's eye and a novelist's perception, Giardina recounts and imagines their evolution from political foes to allies and firm friends, showing "all their flaws" as well as their "basic humanity and basic decency," as she explained to the *Charleston Gazette*. Set against the backdrop of the civil rights movement, Watergate, the Reagan administration, and the second Iraq War, the play offers a searing commentary on contemporary political discourse. *Robert and Ted* debuted with an on-stage reading at FestivALL, an arts celebration in Charleston, West Virginia, in June 2012.

ACT I, SCENE 5

(Multimedia: scenes from the civil rights movement—dogs attacking demonstrators, fire hoses turned on children, marches on the Selma bridge, Dr. Martin Luther King, Jr. speaking.)

Lights up. Byrd is speaking while Kennedy enters and sits at a desk and listens, a look of disgust on his face.

BYRD

And now I'd like to share with the august members of the Senate the society page of the *Welch Daily News*. Mrs. Herman Wells has returned from a trip to visit her daughter in Galax, Virginia. Meanwhile members of the Brooks Garden Club led by Mrs. Charles Lockwood are engaged in a beautification project on the hillside between the train depot and the Veterans' War Memorial Building. They are planting a variety of both annuals and perennials.

KENNEDY

(Stands and claps sarcastically) Congratulations. Fourteen plus hours speaking against the Civil Rights Act, the longest

filibuster in Senate history, and for a great cause. You must be worn out.

CHARLES BOOKER enters and listens.

BYRD

(Tired) Not the longest. That would be Strom Thurmond in 1957.

KENNEDY

Oh, my apologies! Worthy company! Despite Bull Connor and his dogs attacking children in the streets of Birmingham, and those four little girls who were killed in their Sunday school classroom, despite the murder of Negro citizens and civil rights workers across the South. I hoped you might be better than this.

BYRD

(Angry) Of course the murder of civil rights workers is terrible. And those little girls—How dare you accuse me of supporting such atrocities! But the Constitution—

KENNEDY

The courts will decide the constitutionality of this law.

BYRD

The courts will assume we in the Senate have done our job first, and that will sway their ruling. The Constitution gives the right to make these sweeping changes to the states, not the federal government.

KENNEDY

You know, you remind me of those Christians who interpret the Bible literally. We didn't file the Constitution away in a bank vault when the ink dried. The Constitution lives, it breathes, it responds to change. That's its genius.

BYRD

Change should come after people demand it, not because a law forces them to it, and the support for changing race relations just isn't there yet, not in many parts of the country. White people in the South look at all these demonstrations and Negroes getting arrested for openly defying the law and they feel threatened. That's why they accuse Negroes of not knowing their place.

KENNEDY

Tell me, Senator, about a butcher from a coal camp in West Virginia who didn't know his place. Shouldn't you be back in Stotesbury hacking up dead pigs?

Byrd is so furious he is momentarily speechless.

CHARLES BOOKER

(Interrupts) Senator Byrd? Perhaps you'd like to explain to my little boy why the Constitution won't allow him to swim in the city pool back home? Or why, if he gets hungry, a restaurant that serves cheeseburgers isn't his—*(makes imaginary quotation marks in the air)*—place?

BYRD

(Caught by surprise) Who are you?

BOOKER

My name is Charles Booker. From Huntington. I voted for you.

Booker holds out his hand. After a second of hesitation, Byrd shakes it.

BYRD

Tell your little boy— *(He stops, at a loss for words).* You're a taxpayer, aren't you? By rights your little boy should be able to swim in a city pool, but it's up to the City of Huntington to allow that.

BOOKER

You know what the city council tells us? They say if my boy swims in that pool, the white children won't want to swim there.

BYRD

(Uncomfortable) Well, I suppose—I suppose it would be up to the white children, and their parents, whether to swim there or not.

KENNEDY

It will be up to them as soon as we pass this bill. Because the City of Huntington, West Virginia, will have to open its pools to everyone, and citizens like this man won't have to go begging to them.

BYRD

But public facilities are one thing. Private facilities like restaurants and stores—

BOOKER

Last I looked, Senator, there's no white people who need a special membership card to eat a department store cheeseburger.

BYRD

Well, sir. If this Civil Rights legislation passes—*(looks at Kennedy)*—and I believe it will—your son can have his cheeseburger. But wouldn't it be better for all of us if the storeowner offered that place at the table out of the goodness of his heart?

BOOKER

People don't operate that way. I read in the paper you used to be a Sunday School teacher.

BYRD

I was, at the Crab Orchard Baptist Church.

BOOKER

Then you know people, we have some goodness, but we got that meanness in us too. And that's where the government has to step in. To protect people from the meanness. All people.

KENNEDY

Amen.

BYRD

So you've come to Washington to ask me to vote for the Civil Rights bill? I'm sorry, Mr. Booker. I've thought about it long and hard, and I can't do it.

BOOKER

No, sir. That's not why I've come. Of course, I wish you would vote for the Civil Rights bill. But you seem like the kind of person, you'll do what you think you have to.

BYRD

Thank you. *(To Kennedy)* At least my constituents know that.

Kennedy loses interest and wanders to a desk, picks up a document to study.

BOOKER

Even though, sir, *I* think you're wrong.

BYRD

Oh, you do. You don't care to speak your mind, do you?

BOOKER

No, sir, I don't. That's why I'm here. And, for advice.

BYRD

Advice?

BOOKER

That's right. You know more about winning an election in West Virginia than any man alive, as far as I can tell. I'm going to run for Huntington City Council this year. I want to make sure my boy can swim in that pool. And if I win, and serve a term, then I'm going to run for the legislature from Cabell County. There were black people in the West Virginia legislature before, back in the 1920s. Then they disappeared. I think there should be black people down at the Capitol again. Then maybe we can start to change people's minds. Like you said.

BYRD

Black people. Is that the new name for Negroes?

BOOKER

Yes, sir.

BYRD

You all just decided that?

BOOKER

I suppose people can say what they want to be called. Y'all want to be called white, even though you're really kind of pinkish-orange. So now we're black, even though we're all kinds of colors.

BYRD

Humph. *(Thinks a moment)* All right, Mr. Booker. You go on to my office and I'll be along shortly to give you some pointers.

Booker exits. Distant noise of voices speaking. Kennedy has walked to the edge of the stage as though listening. Byrd moves shyly to Kennedy's side.

KENNEDY

Dirksen is speaking now, closing out the debate. *(Listens, then recites what he is hearing) History marches on. It will not be denied. It will not be stayed.*

BYRD

(Repeats Dirksen wistfully) And mankind, thank God, goes forward.

KENNEDY

(Turns to Byrd) Well, some of us do.

BYRD

And Dirksen is a Republican, for heaven's sake. *(Beat)* I'm on the wrong side of history. Aren't I?

KENNEDY

You are.

BYRD

Is that what it means to be a conservative? To always be on the wrong side of history? Because history moves doesn't it, and we're always behind the curve. *(Beat)* I hate change. I can't help it. I want things to stay like—like the good old days.

KENNEDY

Whenever those were.

BYRD

So. I've taken the stands I thought were best. No one was influencing me, I take full responsibility. Now Martin Luther King and those of you who passed the Civil Rights bill will in the future be hailed as heroes. And I will be one of those misguided, forgotten little men who stood in the way.

KENNEDY

(Kennedy studies Byrd for a moment) Don't write your obituary yet. You're too young. All our Southern friends will soon leave the Democrats and cross over to the Republicans. I don't believe you'll be one of them. Because deep inside, you understand the Democrats are the best hope for people of all colors who have no power. *(Looks at his watch)* Well, I'm going to vote. Then I've got a plane to catch, back to Massachusetts.

Kennedy offers Byrd his hand. Byrd looks startled, and then shakes Kennedy's hand. Kennedy exits. STEVE CONRAD enters.

STEVE CONRAD

Senator Byrd. I'm Steve Conrad with the *Washington Star*. I wonder if I might have an interview? A fourteen-hour filibuster! You made your opposition to the new Civil Rights Act pretty clear. Called attention to yourself as well. People in this town are wondering, who is this guy Byrd from Virginia? What makes him tick?

BYRD

I'm not from Virginia. You're thinking of Senator Harry Byrd.

CONRAD

Oh. I thought—*(sifting through the pages of his notebook)*—is there a difference?

BYRD

West Virginia is a separate state. And my name isn't Harry.

CONRAD

(Confused) Well. Senator. People are wondering. Will you pick up the gauntlet of Thurmond and Eastland, the older generation of segregationists? Will you be leaving the Democratic Party, as other white southerners are doing, and join the Republicans?

BYRD

I'm not a southerner.

CONRAD

You're not—*(looks at his notes)* I guess I'm still supposed to interview you.

BYRD

Go ahead.

CONRAD

What's your favorite TV show?

BYRD

Excuse me?

CONRAD

Your favorite television show?

BYRD

(Hesitates, then decides to go along) The only TV I watch is *Gunsmoke*. Now and then.

CONRAD

What do you like to read?

BYRD

Everything. Especially history.

CONRAD

Do you listen to music? What do you think of the Beatles?

BYRD

The—good grief! Sir. Do you really think your readers are interested in this?

CONRAD

To be honest, Senator, I don't know. *(Glances at his notes)* You were a member of the Ku Klux Klan?

BYRD

(Sighs) Yes, I was.

CONRAD

Any comments about that?

BYRD

I have moved past it.

CONRAD

So you renounce—

BYRD

Of course.

CONRAD

But what do they say to you at Washington cocktail parties? Does your Klan membership come up?

BYRD

I don't attend Washington cocktail parties. I don't drink. It's a waste of time. I go home to my wife. I'm away from her enough as it is. So, Mr. Conrad, I don't care what they say about me at Washington cocktail parties.

CONRAD

Well, Senator. *(Beat)* Thanks for remembering my name. *(To himself)* What a weirdo! *(Back to Byrd)* By the way, Senator, did you hear the news? Ted Kennedy's plane crashed on the way home to Massachusetts. The pilot and one of the senator's staff were killed. The senator is in critical condition.

Lights down. ■

UNITED WE STAND DIVIDED WE FALL
KENTUCKY

GOD'S WORK

Blaze had run a septic cleaning company
for fifteen years, called Blaze's Sewer Review.
His emblem? Dead skunk in a crosshairs
above the motto *Dirty deeds done dirt cheap!*
His only son, name Cody, had almost finished
his Associate's in maybe becoming a teacher or a cop,
but now was taking an accidental gap year
where he'd forgot to renew his grants (and made two Ds).
Blaze pretended to be displeased, but truth be told
was happy to have his son around again.
Cody had lived at his mother's house
for almost all of high school, since Blaze
had kept his place outside the good school district.
So Blaze moved back from the hose to the truck cab,
and Cody went to vacuuming up poop, taking back
his sixteenth summer's work for his twenty-first.
The sun was hot and the shit stank
and the pay was never low but it wasn't high
and only certain kinds of women didn't mind
a man who had that station of employment.
But the two made a tolerable living,
and knew where to find those women.
But then that Glade tornado came and tore Glade up.
If nobody had died, it'd have been something to gloat
    about:
two square miles of short circuited crap bombs
and them sitting right there, rolling in it (so to speak).
But people did die, and others wished they had,
and more than that lost Mommy's house and all her things.
The trees looked like the hairline in a razor ad.

So they didn't like the work they took,
and took some cheap, for dinner or beer.
Sometimes they had to do stump removal,
or spend a half day moving furniture
before they got to shoveling out the tank.
They didn't put that on the bill. Almost all
they got paid full for was Jobsite Johnny cleanup,
and it seemed to rain about half of the festivals out.
But nothing was worse than when that church group came
to take the trash and trees from Gladys Lamie's yard.
Jerusalem Church of Jesus the Servant youth group:
twenty-five neon t-shirts strong from St. Jean-Baptiste,
    Iowa.
Everyone picking up trash with one hand, cell phones
in the other; everyone mixing up the names of tools,
asking folks about their accents, not getting jack shit done.
Mrs. Lamie'd double-booked the day; so Blaze and Cody
had to watch all this and try to work around it.
Everything done something they could have done in half
    the time
without the trouble, everything not done something
keeping them from getting to their work.
But the kids were doing God's work, Gladys said;
she held their hands then cried as they prayed for her.
So Blaze and Cody kept their mouths shut for a while
but before the kids were halfway done cleaning
they'd stopped for lunch and pictures.
The girls duckfaced in Jesus name,
with those matching neon shirts: big heart in a house
read *Spreading His love to the whole world!*

Preacher's lady clicked that Nikon camera
while the girls duckfaced and the boys got a chainsaw
stuck in a stump, and flooded out the engine.
Finally it all just ate Blaze up too much.
If a man came in on that stump at angles
he wouldn't have that problem, he hinted to the boys.
Do ya'll want it I could get that out for you?
We're sorry, sir, but we can't let you do that,
the preacher said. *You have to be approved to volunteer.*
Ah, I think we know how to work with tools.
Well all the same, we best get this alone.
And that was all the two said to each other.
The preacher preached and the shovelers shoveled
and neither spoke to the other one again.
But later, heading home, Blaze turned to Cody
and said, *My daddy only ever told me one thing*
about religion: 'You do God's work, but never call it that.'
And that's the only thing I'm going to say to you.

MATT PRATER

CLEARING WITH A MACHETE

For Thor

The early summer swing of a blade
Against brier must not trifle with the
Wiggling ink of a surprised black snake.
Its body will quake as it sings through
The thicket, loops itself through the risky
Puzzle of sapling branch and shivers its tail
In the dead leaves to mimic a timber rattle.
A ferocious deceit, enough to make a man
Circle back with machete on guard.

But this was mere challenge to you, Brave One,
Lion of the lawn, Ajax of the alleyway.
Felis catus, bearing your god's name
With thunderous fare, wrath ruffling your
Eyes and fur as you sprang to ancient war,
Outdoing machete's steel with quick
Tined claws, measuring yourself against
The serpent's fretted strike. Defeat for him
Was written in that morning's haruspicy,
His flight foretold in the curled tendons
Of your Friskies dish.

CHARLES DODD WHITE

AN *APPALACHIAN HERITAGE* INTERVIEW

JACINDA TOWNSEND

In February, Jacinda Townsend's debut novel *Saint Monkey* was published to critical praise. Deeply moving and beautifully written, the book follows two young African-American women as they grow up in Eastern Kentucky in the 1950s. Audrey Martin and Caroline Wallace are consistently confronted with challenges and change; not only must they overcome the tragic loss of beloved family members, but they must do so in a society that subjects them to systemic disadvantages. Their friendship becomes strained when Audrey moves to New York to play piano at the Apollo while Caroline gives up her dream of leaving home and assumes the responsibility of raising her younger sister. *Saint Monkey*, told alternately through the perspectives of both Audrey and Caroline, explores the classic literary theme of growing up and leaving home. The juxtaposition of these two voices results in a powerful work that explores Appalachian identity.

Townsend recently spoke to *Appalachian Heritage* assistant David Cornette about her first novel and Appalachia as a microcosm of America.

■ ■ ■

DAVID CORNETTE: In what ways did growing up in south central Kentucky influence your decision to become a writer?

JACINDA TOWNSEND: I think Kentuckians are great storytellers, and I grew up with a mother and a grandmother who told tremendous stories. It was mostly gossip. [laughs] But the way they gossiped, it always had like a dramatic arc to it. You know, [when you're] just sitting around snapping beans, you can just really learn how to tell great stories.

DC: In the final chapter of the book, Audrey tells a reporter that "a whole language can disappear."

JT: Yeah.

DC: Did you feel an obligation in writing this to present an aspect of Appalachian culture that is disappearing?

JT: Definitely...There are two kind of layers of it. One is just that, part of Appalachian culture, you know, when you're talking about the black people, they were former slaves who were hired to take care of the horses in the area all around Lexington. A lot of those hamlets have either disappeared or shrunk tremendously in size, so in some ways the book was a love letter to that culture that has disappeared. But also to a language that has largely disappeared, so some of the phrases—even some of the syntax and diction of these people—is diction that I heard growing up, and I have not heard since, because those people are literally dying off. You know, my grandmother was the last person I ever heard use the word "nary." So yeah, I wanted to record that.

DC: How did you come to write *Saint Monkey*? Where did the book first begin?

JT: It's actually [the] chapter that's the titular chapter about the murder. That was the first chapter I wrote, so it's loosely based on—there was an actual murder that took place in my hometown. It wasn't really like [in the novel], but it was a domestic murder—a guy killed his wife. And they left behind three kids, and I had always wondered what it was like to be that oldest kid and have to, in effect, raise your sisters...that's how it came to me. And that's how a lot of writing comes to me—I'll see a situation from the outside and wonder what it feels like for the person who's in that situation.

DC: You've said previously that this novel was originally all about Audrey, and told from her point of view. In what ways did the story change by giving Caroline a voice?

JT: Caroline is a lot more bitter; she has a lot more reason to be bitter. And so, in some ways, Caroline is reality, you

Jacinda Townsend

know; Audrey is much more of a dreamer than Caroline is. So when I gave Caroline more of a voice, it changed the story so dramatically because I think the story had been about pursuing your ambition and leaving your home and all those timeless themes, but then the story kind of became about the way people are constrained even when they do follow their dreams.

DC: After spending a few months in New York, Audrey discovers that she's under many of the same limitations that prompted her to leave Kentucky. What does this reflect about the connection between Appalachia and the nation at large?

JT: Well, that Kentucky's really not all that different. [laughs] And I mean, I think it's as true now as it was then, you know. For instance, I lived in New York as an adult; I moved there when I was twenty-three. And I remember a moment, and I was just—I was in the bathroom just like beside myself. I was at work and I went to the bathroom at work and I thought, you know, I have never experienced racism like I have in this workplace, and I had never experienced racism the way I experienced it in New York. In New York it was a very limiting thing, because people were very much defining what you were going to do. I mean, I couldn't even catch a cab in New York; certainly that's not true in Kentucky. And yet, you know, stereotypically we think of Appalachia as this region where a lot of the stereotypes that are put forth in mass media hold true, and it's just not [always the case].

DC: Right.

JT: And so I think it's true, and it was just as true in the fifties [that] women were just as confined in New York as they were in Appalachia. And so people have this idea that "Oh, certain parts of the country are so much more progressive than others," and that's not entirely true. What goes down goes down in different ways depending on where you are.

DC: Another question about Caroline and Audrey—as you mentioned before, they see the world in different ways, despite having a lot in common. Do you identify more closely with either one of them, or do you kind of see them as two separate sides of yourself?

JT: [laughs] That is such a good question. I think another reason that at first I had written more [about] Audrey is that I identified more with her. After I had my second kid and I became a single mother shortly thereafter…I began to really feel, the gender definition in a way that I had not before. I felt like the world was defining me in ways that it had not previously. Caroline, you know, I think that's why she became more of the book too is that there was a part of me that was more Caroline by the time I had finished revising that book. So yeah, [those characters] are two very different sides of me.

DC: Music plays a major role in the plot of *Saint Monkey,* and there also seems to be some tension around the idea of performing music as a job, "just as much as driving a tractor" as you describe it. Could you tell me a little bit about the different ways that music ties into the meaning of the novel?

JT: Sure…I mean, first of all, I always wish that I were a professional musician, and my poor kids [who are musicians] have to—I'm like living through them almost. [laughs] But I also chose that world because I think it's such a metaphor for almost anything that one can do, and it's a really good metaphor. For instance, Audrey's father passes down this gift to her, but it becomes a curse in some ways. You know, it's almost like she's born into this gift she has with music, but she doesn't really know what to do with herself, and so I wanted to kind of think about that. But also because, oh my gosh, it was such a—when I started doing the research of the jazz world of the fifties—what a rich tapestry to explore. And it was also a way to talk about just what the fifties were socially and politically.

DC: The novel ends at a time in which society begins to undergo major changes, and yet the last lines are whispered words from the past. What is the effect of emphasizing this recurrent memory amidst a quickly changing world?

JT: One thing that is happening to Audrey is that she's realizing...that when you leave a place, it is not just about you individually leaving a place. When you leave a place, you are very much using that to continue a way of life...It's almost like when people immigrate here from other countries—when you leave a part of this country that has such a rich, rich culture, you're choosing—in some ways, you're choosing not to be a part of that anymore. You can continue it all you want, you know—there's this scene where she's like "I have to go get that salt for the house, cause that's what my daddy told me to do for good luck." You can take it with you but you are, in fact, choosing not to be a part of it. And in having these memories—and I know you talked about the last scene, and that's the memory of her being with August—but I think that's what a lot of her memory is, and I think it may also be the author's kind of memory and wistful longing to have continued her own culture.

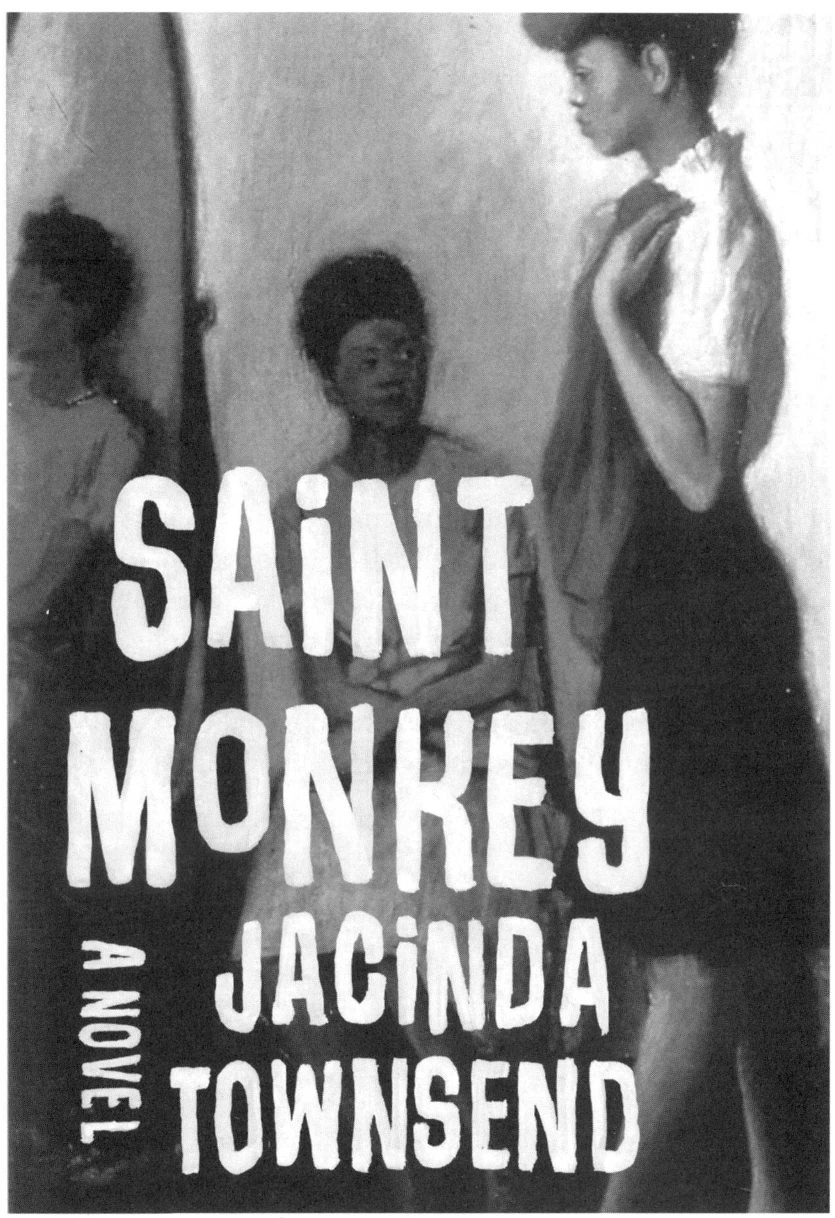

Upon its publication in February, *Saint Monkey* was hailed as "a gorgeously realized novel of cruelty and sorrow" in a starred review by *Booklist* and a "compelling debut" in the *New York Times* Sunday Book Review.

DC: What piece of writing advice do you like to give to all of your students?

JT: Stay in the game. It's a game—the Yankees, you know, if you think about it, actually lose sixty percent of the games that they play—and they're a phenomenal team, right? And so it's the same with writing—it's just a job. And I like to tell this story but my students don't like to hear it, but when I sold this novel my second kid was four months old, and I was talking to the editor and I had this child who had just pooped and gone to sleep. [laughs] So she had a dirty diaper and I was just praying through the phone call that she wouldn't wake up, and I got off the phone and I just changed her diaper, so there was no fifty-yard line dance or anything like that. Because I've always felt that if you get really dejected by failure, you also have to be really invested in success, and neither thing is good for writing, because writing really is—you have to stay in the game. You have to keep doing it; it's a job. And that's the way I like to think of it: "I'm gonna get up and do this no matter what." ■

THE INTIMACY OF SPOONS

Knives with serrated edges, their solid singularity
    and sureness of purpose;

Forks too with fang teeth
and slots of air,
their habit of piercing—

Neither will ever know
the intimacy of spoons.

How they hold each other—
knees cupped, thighs touching,

the long curve of spine
soft against belly and chest,

the nuzzled narrow neck,
this ladle of bodies.

Slowly your breathing softens, falls
into that space of sleep

where you twitch in dreams
and I hold on.

JIM MINICK

LOOKING INSIDE

KAREN SALYER MCELMURRAY

"There was a time," says Neil Genzlinger in a January 2011 article in the *New York Times*, "when you had to earn the right to draft a memoir, by accomplishing something noteworthy or having an extremely unusual experience or being such a brilliant writer that you could turn relatively ordinary occurrences into a snapshot of a broader historical moment. Unremarkable lives went unremarked upon, the way God intended." When, this article asks us, is portrayal of a life on the page merely "oversharing," to the tune of 160,000 hits in an average Google search? "Memoirs," Genzlinger continues, "have been disgorged by virtually everyone who has ever had cancer, been anorexic, battled depression, lost weight…taught an underprivileged child, adopted an underprivileged child or been an under-privileged child. By anyone who was raised in the '60s, '70s or '80s, not to mention the '50s, '40s or '30s. Owned a dog. Run a marathon. Found religion. Held a job."[1]

I admit it: as a memoirist, I bristled when I read this article. My teeth clenched and I paced. Listen here, buddy. Listen to what memoirist Sue William Silverman had to say in a recent editorial called "In Defense of Memoir: Once More into the Fray":

> To write a memoir is not a simple act of regurgitation or spitting out facts to an 'interesting story' along the lines of 'first this happened to me, then this happened, then this next thing happened.' Of much greater interest, and at the heart of memoir, is the story behind the story, the memoirist's courageous ability to reflect upon the past, thus artistically recasting his or her experience into one that's transformative.[2]

1 Neil Genzlinger, "The Problem with Memoirs," *The New York Times*, January 28, 2011, http://www.nytimes.com/2011/01/30/books/review/Genzlinger-t.html.

2 Sue William Silverman, "In Defense of Memoir," *Brevity*, September 8, 2011, http://brevity.wordpress.com/2011/09/08/in-defense-of-memoir.

3 Christopher Lasch, *The Culture of Narcissism: American Life in an Age of Diminishing Expectations* (New York: W. W. Norton & Company, 1991), 3; Silverman, "In Defense of Memoir."

4 Patricia Hampl, *I Could Tell You Stories: Sojourns in the Land of Memory* (New York: W. W. Norton & Company, 2000), 35.

The truth? I agree with some of what Neil Genzlinger says in his essay. But I'd like to put aside for a while the question of memoir as potentially problematic and focus instead on why, in this often overly self-referential world of Facebook and Twitter, of reality shows and blogs—and of what Christopher Lasch says in *The Culture of Narcissism* is the massive "social invasion of the self"—we still need an art form that demands that we look deeply inside ourselves, both as writers and readers, as writers of fiction and nonfiction, as writers who believe in that "courageous ability" to transform experience into those mysterious marks on the page called words.[3]

■ ■ ■

"True memoir," says essayist Patricia Hampl in her essay "Memory and Imagination," "is written in an attempt to find not only a self, but a world."[4] Finding is a journey, one essential to writing both fiction and creative nonfiction. The journey of

...we still need an art form that demands that we look deeply inside ourselves, both as writers and readers, as writers of fiction and nonfiction...

writing good prose involves not only a manipulation of craft elements but also the uncovering, in draft after draft, of the true heart of a piece at hand. As a writer, I firmly believe that until we ask those hard questions of our prose and of our own lives, our work, as fiction writer Dorothy Allison says, "won't be worth a damn."

I'd like to tell a story—my own story of reaching for these difficult questions as I've moved from the writing of a novel, to the writing of a memoir, and back again to fiction. In my particular journey, one art form has been absolutely essential to the writing of another. To understand one form, I've entered another, then journeyed back again, in my search for greater depth in my characters and their insights, in my plots and their complexities. I call this journey "looking inside."

■ ■ ■

My journey as a writer began with houses. Houses made of the blood and bones and lives of the women in my mother's family. Pearlie, Ruby, Ruth. Women who have all lived their lives in Floyd County in Eastern Kentucky. Houses. Ghosts of houses. Houses beset by fire, births, deaths. Open doors, shut doors. Houses you enter and never leave.

Over thirty years ago, Pearlie Lee, my mother, went to live in a house off State Road 1498 in Lancer, Kentucky. In that house, she clipped my granny's nails, braided her long hair, bathed her. She seldom left that house at all unless her brother drove her five miles up the road to the small town of Prestonsburg. Once her parents died, my mother was alone and soon adrift in the early stages of dementia. For years she decorated her dead mother's walker with plastic flowers. She sat alone at night, brushed her teeth for precisely half an hour, did forty minutes of laps through the immaculate rooms past an enlarged photo of Ruby, her dead sister.

That sister lived her last years in an apartment building for the handicapped, though her greatest handicap, as I recall it, was simply being afraid. In an eight-floor concrete apartment building with a guard rail along the halls and a persistent smell of something medicinal and sanitary, Ruby woke from dreams of a Holy Ghost with her own face, a ghost who lifted her up into the safety of madness. The third sister, Ruth, the youngest, still lives up Mining Hollow, outside of Prestonsburg. She spends her days tending house and the grave of her son, which she can see from her trailer's kitchen window. Like Ruby and my mother, Ruth also leaves home less and less since her son's suicide, a self-inflicted gunshot in the back room of the trailer. When I visited there one August, Ruth's husband was leaving to go squirrel hunting. Just joking, he waved his rifle in the air, pointed it at us. From the couch, Ruth said, *I can't stand it when you do that.* She didn't get up.

It haunts me, that world I've come to see as governed by an unkind God, a father-god, not the real lives of women. When I think of their lives I think of Mildred Haun's *The Hawk's Done Gone*, a collection of stories set in the east Tennessee mountains. The women in Haun's stories say, again and again, "I should have knowed," meaning "should have known" the events that led to deaths, despair, loss, should have known, but couldn't, couldn't act, even with knowledge of events right at hand. I think of Ruby, Ruth and Pearlie, and I think of houses, curtains drawn tight at all times of day, inexplicable rules that keep them safe. Used to be, when I walked up the steps to visit my mother in her house, I'd see her peering out, face hidden by a door screen or a curtain. Houses keep the world at bay.

My mother is just one of my ghosts of Eastern Kentucky. Her ghost, all the ghosts of Eastern Kentucky, its graves and houses, its possibilities and impossibilities, find me when I settle down to that mystery called writing. Where exactly am I in this house of bones and blood, this inheritance of women's lives? In my writing journal, my dreams often best tell the story of my writing world. In one dream, I was at a table in my mother's house, on the day of my dead grandmother's surgery. Ruby and my mother and I were eating a mountain salad drizzled with bacon grease, and the house, uncharacteristically, was in a chaos of unwashed dishes and clothes. Asking about this in my dream, I was told that we were all moving to a house made of glass.

My own writing self is sometimes as fragile as that—an inheritance of depression, vulnerability. My psyche's house, sometimes haunted by fear of my own language. From a journal from a few years ago: *Want to write; can't, can't. When I read my writing, it's by someone else altogether. Give my writing back to me.*

Nineteenth-century American writer Harriet Spofford's story, "Circumstance," is beautifully and painfully about women and their "owning" of their own voices. In the first pages of Spofford's story, we know that the protagonist is a woman on the brink of "a death...worse than any other that is to be named." She is a frontier woman who spends an entire winter night held captive in a tree by a panther. To stay alive, she sang to him all night long. But does the protagonist own her own songs? At every turn there is a "he" in this story: baby with his plump fists, husband with his "stalwart and strong" presence, the Lord with his "judgments...in all the earth," panther with his "long red tongue."[5] This story's singer translates nursery songs, hymns, love ballads from a tradition she does not own. By the end her husband rescues her from the panther, and we enter her dream of a house set fire and her own soul rising over the flames.

Ownership was the question I confronted in 1997, when I'd at last completed a novel called *Strange Birds in the Tree of Heaven*. The book is partly about a woman named Ruth Blue, her childhood abandonment by her mother and her difficult coming to womanhood. Like the women in my own family, Ruth's life also is a story of loss, powerlessness and even madness—schizophrenic visions, agoraphobia. Ruth's greatest obsession, and the novel's plot, is her son's, Andrew's, love for

5 Harriet Prescott Spofford, "Circumstance," in *The Amber Gods and Other Stories*, ed. Alfred Bendixen (New Brunswick: Rutgers University Press, 1989), 270, 272, 274, 276.

another boy. Ruth is convinced that if she can save Andrew from this love, she will be able to offer him her vision of God instead. Ruth Blue dreams of god as a "woman without a face" and of the man she will love, also with a face she "could never clearly see." By letting go of this world and reaching for the next one, Ruth imagines herself, "lighter and lighter, rising over all the earth she has ever known." At one moment, dreaming of a bombing in France during World War I, she dreams of her own death, that body of "arms and legs at strange angles, a stick figure drawn with pencil." By the end of the novel, Ruth Blue is held fast to the only earth she's ever known—Eastern Kentucky,

My own writing self is sometimes as fragile as that—an inheritance of depression, vulnerability.

Mining Hollow, the house of her father, the house of God. Ruth Blue's voice is only powerful when she envisions the world cleansed by fire, made new again with her own son's death.

Behind this fictive world are ghosts of real people and events. Ruth Blue is my mother's sister, Ruth. Andrew is a combination of her late son, my cousin Greg, and another Eastern Kentucky boy I once knew, one called "an abomination in the eyes of God" because of his love for men. The climactic night in the lives of my novel was the night on which the real Ruth went out to get the shotgun with which my drunken cousin killed himself. The events made me and I made a novel that took me years to finish, so painful was the building of words, the exploring of a psychic house. The story moved inside me, held fast by the real world and its stories, a ghost beneath dark waters.

■ ■ ■

For a while after I finished *Strange Birds in the Tree of Heaven*, I *was* Ruth Blue. I was in the throes of darkness. As Natalia Ginzburg says in an essay called "My Vocation," I had entered a dark world with my writing, one "filled with echoes and trembling and shadows, [one] to which [I was] bound by a devout and passionate pity."[6]

I was in the grips of depression. I'd always found that phrase amusing with its evocations of gigantic hands reaching down out of heaven. Now I wasn't laughing.

My writing life was reduced to lists. Grocery lists. Lists of papers to grade for my new teaching job at the local college. Lists of tasks. Lawns to mow and rent to pay and committee meetings to attend. Occasionally, I'd dip into some popular self-help book suggesting list-making as a way to enter the subconscious and emerge again, scathed but healed. Make a list, the book would suggest, of the ten most important events to shape your experiences until now. I wrote down how I saw the ocean for the first time when I was eighteen and the time I hiked forty-four miles across the Grand Canyon, there and back. I listed events one through five, but after that all the other blank lines in my empty notebook left me shaking. Words themselves left me empty and frightened. Some evenings, I found that I simply couldn't stop crying.

I agree with Ginzburg when she says "you cannot hope to console yourself for your grief by writing."[7] But it was writing that began to save me. At first, post-novel, I wrote almost nothing. I kept a dream journal. I worked at the revision of some short stories. Then, mid-winter—I think of that time as a kind of perennial winter—I began to take a hard look, again, at *Strange Birds* in its manuscript form. Accompanying that draft was a piece I'd written when I was just finishing graduate school, an apologia that accompanied my creative dissertation.

As I looked back at this piece, I reread what I'd said about writers who influenced my work and what I'd said about craft and process, but more than that, I began to see more clearly what I'd written about the influences on my work of the women in my family. And somewhere, in the middle of those pages about those women, I found a few sentences I'd written about my own life. I'd described a dream I'd had once, when I was traveling in Crete and sleeping out on a beach at night. I'd described how, in the middle of the night as I slept, a blond-haired boy came up out of the sea and walked toward me, touched the top of my head. *It's all right,* he said. *I forgive you.*

And so I began again to write. I filled pages with stories I remembered and with hard questions. What, I wanted to know, had caused my mother's descent into fear? Why had she gone back to her parent's house in Eastern Kentucky and never left?

As I wrote more during two summers at an artist's retreat in North Georgia, I began to realize that the real story still wasn't being told. I looked again at the essay, and at that blond-haired boy who walked up out of the ocean began to appear again in my dreams. Sometimes he looked like his father, the boy I'd married and divorced by the time I was eighteen and other times he looked like me, in photographs of myself at the Lynch, Kentucky, elementary school when I was six. It was necessary, I was beginning to realize, to go deeper—to enter the real house of consciousness. I needed to look not just at the women I'd grown up with, but at the woman I had, at over forty-years-old, not yet become. I was a woman who feared intimacy, who wanted children but had never had them, who grew depressed in late June, early July. I was a woman who had begun to wake herself up at night with uterine contractions. I want no children, I'd told friends for years. I

6 Natalia Ginzburg, *The Little Virtues* (New York: Arcade Publishing, 1989), 66.

7 Ibid.

want, I told them, books. I want to write. But at what cost? "Our capacity to move forward as developing beings rests on a healthy relationship with the past," writes Patricia Hampl.[8] A wall of forgetting had stood between me and my own loss.

The doors of memory began to open as for the next three years I worked on what later became my memoir, *Surrendered Child,* the story of my relinquishment of a child to a state-supported adoption in Kentucky. I wrote a dream I'd had about the apocalypse during the forty-eight hours of my labor with my son's birth. I wrote the taste of sweet yellow milk from my own breasts, and how my breasts dried and ached and emptied after I'd given him up. I wrote my son's birth, his surrender, and not quite miraculously, as I wrote, my depression shifted, curled itself up inside me, a smaller creature I could begin to live with. My writing was becoming, as a friend has described it, "beautiful pain." I began to think of it as the translation of darkness, and it was a language I was beginning to understand.

■ ■ ■

In the documentary *The Rough South of Harry Crews,* Crews talks, as he does in his memoir, *Childhood: An Autobiography of a Place,* about the life that informed much of his work. Poverty in the farmland of Bacon County, Georgia. An alcoholic uncle he grew up believing was his father. Two major childhood illnesses, one a paralysis that left the muscles in his legs so contracted they pulled his heels up along his back. Three years as a Marine in Korea. All of this preceding his first writing workshop at the University of Florida, where his mentor, Andrew Lytle, took barely a look at the story's first paragraph—flung it back at Crews with the advice to, "burn it, son. Fire's a great refiner." Still, as Crews tells us late in the film, he "does not want to get caught saying that a life of hardship builds character any more than it makes the work what it needs to be."[9]

Like Crews, I don't want to get caught saying that we need hardship in order to be better people, better writers. But I do know that memoir takes courage, and that courage is a necessary ingredient to the writing life. This courage is about reaching into the depths, into structure and shape, into point of view and characterization, into language in all ways.

Writing a memoir was, perhaps first and foremost, a lesson for me in shape. In the first place, as Hampl says, "the

My writing was becoming, as a friend had described it, "beautiful pain."

story seems to be already there, already accomplished and fully achieved in history."[10] This was absolutely the case for me. With the writing of a novel, I struggled to achieve narrative shape—how the plot should "move" forward, especially since I'd chosen a complicated pattern. I'd attempted to place chapters about one night against another series of forward-moving chapters that begin in the early 1900s. On top of that, the narrative shifts between each of three major narrators. In short, the structure was a complicated one. Writing the memoir, on the other hand, forced me to look at one story, my own, and one "plot trajectory." That plot helped me focus in the craft sense, on basic choices, among them: time (when to begin the telling of my story and when to end

8 Hampl, 33.

9 *The Rough South of Harry Crews*. TV. Directed by Gary Hawkins. University of North Carolina Center for Public Television, 1992.

10 Hampl, 24.

it); flashback (how to incorporate the past and when and how much), and which parts of the story to relate as scene and which as summary. All of these questions about time are heightened with the writing of a memoir, because the writer must shape a *life* into narrative and must make, accordingly, enormous decisions about which events are crucial to that narrative and when and in what proportion.

Characterization would seem, naturally, a far easier matter for the memoirist—after all, a memoir is one's own story. Not necessarily true. Just as with plot, character presents a complex and instructive craft lesson. In the first place, the obvious truth is that I'm writing *myself.* I know myself. Or do I? For the work of characterization to be done well, I must step outside of my own experience, examine that experience as if it belongs to a character I'm creating, one that can be entered, recognized, seen by the reader; I must become a character. I must become a physical presence in the narrative.

I also discovered that one can choose point of view, and this has surprised me, perhaps most of all. One can choose a combination of first, second, first person plural and third person points of view. Or one could choose a very close limited third person, as Sonya Huber did in *Opa Nobody,* a narrative in which she enters the consciousnesses of her great-grandfather and her grandfather to tell their stories of political resistance in Germany. But my particular models for point of view for my memoir were Mary Karr's *The Liar's Club,* and *Cherry,* its sequel. I was interested in structure in *The Liar's Club,* and in Karr's use of second person in alternating chapters in *Cherry.*

The second person, which I use in some places in my memoir, can have several effects. I can "address" the reader, and include them more directly in my very personal story. Second person can also function as "the self" addressing self—

me providing a kind of inner voice to address myself about my own experiences. Needless to say, point of view, and the effects on characterization, is tantamount to a mind-blowing, vision quest. Who is who, in the end? What I hope for, when the draft is written, is what Bret Lott describes in his essay, "Toward a Definition of Creative Nonfiction." Lott calls the "proactive element of creative nonfiction" the fact that it forces us to take "responsibility as human beings...to answer for and to our lives."[11] To become a fully rounded character in one's own story necessitates such responsibility—and I can only hope for the benefits for my own life, not to mention the lives of characters I am and hope to write in the world of fiction.

Finally, my experiences with shaping life into narrative art have most importantly of all made me further examine the sheer *meaning* of stories in general, be they fiction or creative nonfiction. Patricia Foster, in her essay "The Intelligent Heart," says that creative nonfiction, truth-telling in writing, can lead us to "stories [that] come from the mystery of unknowable places...[a] summons [that] must be untangled and distilled, worked like the unraveling of a rope, piece by piece, thread by thread, then put together with the embrace of two broken thumbs." True knowledge, which comes from the intelligent heart, is as Foster says "the source, the goods, the first principle from which everything else is made."[12] Whether we are making stories on our own pages, or helping others cultivate those pages for themselves in the workshop, I've come to believe that we must enter the center, the deep cave, the unknown mystery, of the self.

11 Bret Lott, "Toward a Definition of Creative Nonfiction" in *Before We Get Started: A Practical Memoir of the Writer's Life* (New York: Ballantine, 2005), 90.

12 Patricia Foster, "The Intelligent Heart," *The Fourth Genre: Contemporary Writers of/on Creative Nonfiction*, eds. Robert L. Root, Jr. and Michael Steinberg (New York: Pearson Longman, 2005), 304.

■ ■ ■

In a March 25, 2005 issue of the online *New York Times*, critic William Grimes addresses what he sees as a "glut" in the market for memoirs, wondering how it is that "the genre has become so inclusive that it's almost impossible to imagine which life experiences do not qualify as memoir material."[13]

I agree with Grimes to some extent. I too have read substantial number of memoirs in the last few years, and have come to approach them with an attitude reminiscent of Glenda in *The Wizard of Oz,* who in this case asks: *are you a good memoir, or a bad memoir?* The good ones, for me, are multi-layered with their characterizations, their plots, and their meanings. And I've been surprised and disappointed with a few others.

Whether a book is creative nonfiction or fiction, I want the story to lift off the page, to transcend itself. To use the language of poets, I want the vehicle (the story) to pack a real tenor (the larger meaning). In "Circumstance" as the protagonist is being held captive in a tree at night by a panther, she thinks, "Let us be ended by fire…[be] ashes, for the winds to bear, the leaves to cover; let us be ended by wild beasts, and the base, cursed thing howls with us forever through the forest...and what force [this knowledge] lent to her song..."[14] I want books I love to be this kind of song, strong enough to bear us away from our very own selves. In the purely intuitive sense, I just *feel* a book when it's powerful, especially the story of a life well-told.

Unfortunately, the telling of lives has been just the problem I've encountered over the years. As far back as an undergraduate poetry class at Berea College, I remember being told that discussion of poems by Anne Sexton and Sylvia Plath would take up less class time, since they were "merely confessional." A few years ago, I was riding in a van from AWP in Palm Springs, to LAX. In the van were several other writers from various programs across the country, and they were talking about a job search they'd be doing for a "creative nonfiction hire." It was new to me that there were rankings of type for such a job—travel writing ranked higher than nature writing, which ranked higher than a memoir. "Personal stories," one woman said, "just wouldn't be taken as seriously."

Then there's a 1997 *Vanity Fair* article by James Walcott, who had this to say: "Creative writing and creative nonfiction are coming together, I fear, to form a big earnest blob of

Whether a book is creative nonfiction or fiction, I want the story to lift off the page, to transcend itself.

me-first sensibility...a sickly transfusion, whereby the weakling personal voice of sensitive fiction is inserted into the beery carcass of nonfiction."[15] As Lee Gutkind, the editor of the journal *Creative Nonfiction* says, "Wolcott boils down all creative nonfiction into what he calls 'confessional writing' and takes to task as 'navel gazers' nearly any writer who had been the lest bit self-revelatory in their work."[16]

13 William Grimes, "We All Have a Life. Must We All Write About It?", *The New York Times*, March 25, 2005, http://www.nytimes.com/2005/03/25/books/25memo.html.

14 Spofford, 272.

15 James Wolcott, "Me, Myself, and I," *Vanity Fair*, October 1997, 214.

16 Diego X. Jesus and Mark London, "New New Journalism: Lee Gutkind Gets Real," *Inkwell Newswatch*, January 2008, http://www.fwointl.com/artman/publish/article_695.shtml.

Finally, of course, there's the article that prompted this essay. For Neil Genzlinger, memoir is "an absurdly bloated genre," but for the sake of his article he read four new ones. "Three of the four," he says, "did not need to be written, a ratio that probably applies to all memoirs published over the last two decades." Along the way of this laborious reading journey, Genzlinger did, I discovered, come up with some really good, and very valuable advice for those who survive the test of the reading public and choose to write in this form after all. Here are Genzlinger's Guidelines:

1. "The prose isn't particularly surprising, and, more to the point, neither is the selection of anecdotes: cheerleader tryouts, crummy teenage jobs and, that favorite of oversharers everywhere, the loss of virginity."

2. "That's what happens when immature writers write memoirs: they don't realize that an ordeal, served up without perspective or perceptiveness, is merely an ordeal."

3. "If you still must write a memoir, consider making yourself the least important character in it."

4. "There can't be just one book by a bulimic or former war correspondent or spouse of an Alzheimer's sufferer; there has to be a pile."

5. "But they are lost in a sea of people you've never heard of, writing uninterestingly about the unexceptional, apparently not realizing how commonplace their little wrinkle is or how many other people have already written about it."

6. "No, the sole purpose of this memoir, like many, many others concerning some personal trial, is to generate sympathy for its author."[17]

■ ■ ■

In my writing classes these days, I have become something of a zealot. The most important part of the writing life, I tell my students, isn't a workshop or craft discussion. The real writing life isn't about publication. It's about transcendence, I tell them. It's about the times spirit is at work. It's how the poet Alice Friman describes the creating of a poem. *A ghost in the bones.* What, I ask the students, transcends even us when we put words down on a page? Some of the students are on to me, my single-mindedness. "I've tried transcendence," a student a few terms back told me when I pushed her to go deeper in an essay I required a class to write about the process of making their stories and poems and essays. "And it didn't work."

And yet I hold on to my beliefs and my insistence upon them for my workshops. I wholeheartedly believe, as Charles Baxter says in *The Art of the Subtext*, that "what starts at the intimately personal [level] eventually enlarges." Mere words, charged with the large task of conveying the transcendent, the larger than, the message. Writing, what Baxter calls gazing into the "face of the Other." The Other? In my writing life "Other" means our own least understood self, the face of the beloved, the face of God even. It means striving for, as best we can with our own human hands, an *I and Thou* relationship with our language. Words charged with responsibility in an age, again as Baxter says, of "epistemological skepticism, irony, cynicism, the ability to be in on the joke, and our occasional wish, knowing there is no center, to be swept away."[18]

17 Genzlinger, "The Problem with Memoirs."

18 Charles Baxter, *The Art of Subtext: Beyond Plot* (Minneapolis: Graywolf Press, 2007), 173, 151.

Writing memory, has made me at least glimpse a center. "Memoir," as Patricia Hampl says, "seeks a permanent home for feeling and image, a habitation where they can live together."[19] With the writing of fiction (a story in part about the loss of the relationship of a parent and child), I wrote images, evoked feelings that eventually found their home in the real story that lay ahead—the meeting with my son. And more than that, as I turn again to the pages of fiction, after having written a memoir, I've discovered a self I can live with, and a pervasive sense of the possibility of creating language, in fiction and nonfiction, that drinks from the Twin Rivers of joy and of sorrow. At least that's the truth I'm still discovering. ■

19 Hampl, 29.

FLEA MARKET TREASURE

Turned out in her finest frock,
she squints into the sun, poses
stiff-spined for the camera,
smiling for this souvenir portrait,
now faded, enigmatic sepia.
Rocky Mountains rise behind her,
and I imagine a visit to the Wild West
gravesite of Buffalo Bill, panorama
of golden prairie and the jutting
hogbacks of earth's backbone,
hot, dry wind tugging tendrils
of hair out of its tight bun.
She holds a ten-gallon hat,
perhaps the photographer's prop.
No man's arm encumbers her waist,
no child peeps from behind skirts.
This postcard, clean as a new slate—
memento of her first trip to a land
unlike the enclosing Blue Ridge,
or proof of independence—
no address, no postmark telling time
or place, no trace of looping cursive
wish you were here.

JANICE HORNBURG

PHYLLIS DILLON
ONE LIFE TO LIVE
SIDE 2
1430 K
ONE LIFE TO LIVE
TIME IS ON MY SIDE

NOT THE MOUNTAIN KIND

RACHEL GARRINGER

They broke down in the thick hot air on the side of the highway in Arkansas. It was a big old boat of a Buick, deer tan. Leroy had bought it for $100 and then rebuilt the engine. He couldn't read, but when he closed his eyes he could trace the workings of an engine from start to finish in his mind. His old lady was asleep, swollen and pregnant with his first child in the passenger seat. Her baby from her last man was asleep, too, on her lap. Both of them were red and sticky in the heat. There was the sound of mosquitoes whining and the slap of his hands against their bites. The big rigs barreled by much faster now that they sat still with the bright green of the rice paddies laid out alongside them.

He wondered where she dreamed of when she slept; the mountains of their home or the hot plains of her youth outside Texarkana where they were headed. He'd never left West Virginia before, except to go to the part of Virginia that might as well have seceded with them in 1863. From what he'd seen so far, he figured he wouldn't have any reason to ever leave home again, assuming they made it back. He woke her to tell her that the car was dead and he was going for help. She scowled and said, "Goddammit, Leroy!" and then closed her eyes again. He left his woman, her child, and their unborn baby sleeping in the car in the slow afternoon, and set out walking, long left arm outstretched, muscles distinct beneath tanned skin, thumb up towards the sky.

The woman who picked him up drove a new Toyota, talked clean and harsh like people in the movies do. She said she was from New York City, on her way back to Austin, wrapping up a tour. There were guitars in hard black cases in the back seat, coated in stickers. There was fine blond hair on her legs above her cowboy boots, and a tattoo peeking out from the neckline of her shirt. He could hear her bracelets clinking like the wind chimes on his mother's porch as she turned up the air conditioning. She asked him lots of questions, but he kept his mouth closed as much as possible without being rude, not wanting to let his rounded words out into the air with her sharp ones.

"Have you ever been to Clifftop?" she asked. "I go every year." The festival that young kids with money went to over near Sam Black Church where the girls didn't wear bras, and the boys wore thick beards and flannel shirts but talked like this woman, and they all took drugs but never got busted. He remembered how a young girl in an old fashioned dress had flirted with his Uncle after she heard him play the banjo. And how his sister had pulled at her own shirt hem and fidgeted around all those young women whose teeth and hair and skin glowed, who carried themselves with such importance. He remembered how they'd ignored her, hadn't even looked at her, even though she was the best fiddler there. How it had made him want to fight someone, and he had, and then his whole family had gotten kicked out. They'd never gone back.

"No ma'am," he replied.

She finally stopped asking him questions, and turned up a Hazel and Alice recording. She sang along with a voice like powdered sugar: flexible and pretty, sweet and white. He could tell life had gone easy on her. He bet she hadn't bought the car with money earned making music. He heard his mama's voice in his head saying, "You can't sing a mountain song unless you know despair up close and personal." He thought

He could hear her bracelets clinking like the wind chimes on his mother's porch as she turned up the air conditioning.

of his brother and sister sitting on upturned buckets on the patio outside the trailer, singing and picking, the crickets and katydids joining in on the harmony. He felt his throat tighten. Felt a deep gratefulness wash over him for all that he'd lived through. Maybe he couldn't ever be free of folks who thought they were better than him, but at least he understood a few things about living, about surviving, about despair. It was only when this woman's car faded off into the distance, and he breathed down deep into the bottom of his lungs, that he realized he'd near to suffocated on the ride.

The mechanic told him it'd cost $400 to fix something he knew was only worth $150, even with labor. So he walked in the direction the man had told him to, till he got to the junkyard out on the edge of town. He heard the roar as he was trying to argue down the price of the part he needed. Everything stopped: the birds, the wind, the sound of his own voice. He walked away still holding the part though he hadn't paid, and rounded a mountain of flattened cars. The junkyard owner shouted after him "Wouldn't go over there if I was you, boy, less you're looking to get ate."

It was an African lion, with a full mane, not the mountain kind from back home. Its hair had fallen out in thick patches, and there was a dullness to its golden eyes despite the strength of its voice. It snarled, but still he walked closer. "What the fuck are you doing? You stupid boy," the junkyard owner yelled at him again. But Leroy walked closer yet, arm outstretched, palm facing skyward, until he could feel the lion's breath against it. He could see the sunlight trapped inside the mane, though dust and malnutrition had muted its glow. Its whiskers spread out and towards him, ears forward and alert. It tilted its chin up.

The lion's nose was dry like sandpaper against his palm. It opened its mouth to lick his hand just as the junkyard man's whip cracked against its hips. It roared and ran, cowered against the post where it was chained, bleeding and hissing. He saw dark scars crisscrossing its back, and dog food thrown on the ground right next to where it shit.

"I don't know how women raise you up in West Virginia," the junkyard man said with malice in his voice, "but in Arkansas boys are raised to listen."

Leroy bought the part for more than it was worth, wanting to get away from the junkyard man and quick, knowing that if the man called him boy one more time he'd lose it. If there was one thing he'd learned in life it was that if he waited too long to walk away, he was liable to not find a way out. He walked back up the road the same way he'd come, facing the cars and trucks that sped past, eyes to the ground. He couldn't shake the image of that lion, bleeding and hissing.

■ ■ ■

As a boy, in the mornings, when the sun was still hidden by the eastern mountains, he had gone down to the river with the mountain lions to swim. The sun had shone through the high point on the ridge where the big spruce had fallen, and through the low gap where he'd cross over to the store when he awoke before his siblings to find the house empty of food. Other than those two stripes of light, the bottom was dark, and thick fog hung close to the water's surface.

Jim and Julie McClain, the owners of the small zoo over the hill from his home, had paid him two dollars a day for exercising the lions and bears, cleaning out their pens, and changing their water. The McClains had always been an odd lot, since back to Civil War times at least, when it was rumored that Jim McClain's great-granddaddy had fought for both sides at the Battle of Droop Mountain; periodically running across the open firing range butt naked with his muzzle loader held high. So no one was surprised when Jim started trapping young mountain lions and bears, and charging tourists money to see them.

The old feline had been Leroy's favorite, stoic and glowing. She would sit in the far corner of her pen and watch him approach. He had always wondered if some day she would pounce down on him when he opened the heavy wooden door. Once he had opened it she would slink down off of her high platform and walk slowly towards him; touch his hand with her cool flat nose, and the shape of her eyes would change, letting him know it was okay to clip the lead to the ring in her collar. She had walked slowly and regally beside him on the mowed path down to the rocky shore. When they'd passed through the woods he could feel her, alert with every inch of her lean body. He'd tried to imitate what she did, to sense the forest without seeing it straight on, through that part of himself that most people have all but left behind, the part that knows things without the guidance of senses.

At the river's edge he would unclip the lead, strip down to his boxers, and dive into the cool water. She would sit on the bank and watch him, as a mother would. After some time, she would sniff the water's surface, test it with the tip of one large paw and tiptoe in gingerly, before the final ungraceful splash. Then she would swim across, muscles rippling below her skin as the water rolled over, the currents not seeming to faze her. She'd swim out towards the thick forest on the far bank, towards the wild, towards her freedom. But always, she would turn back, swim past him, and rise out of the water all skin and bones. And then the long bath, the self-involved preening would commence, where she licked herself thoroughly, and then dozed in the warm sun which had by then peaked the ridge.

That had been in high school, when he had been saving back his two dollars a day for the '72 El Camino, navy blue with glitter flake that Bill had for sale at his shop down by the Dairy Queen. It was only fifteen years old and had 3,000 miles on it, and he had known that once he had that car he'd finally be free. He'd earned extra money on the side fixing cars and tractors. The El Camino had sold to a rich man from Charleston passing through on business. An old farmer had given Leroy a '67 Chevy truck that was all but rusted through in the frame, saying "Boy, you're 'bout the only one I know who could fix it, and needs it bad enough to try."

That had also been before Leroy had got into trouble, before he'd moved into town with his Uncle Dill, who seemed always to hover at death's door. The alcohol hadn't pickled his uncle and preserved him, but had instead made him into a grey shell of a man. Soon after moving in Leroy had burned the lady cop's house down, the one some said took women home at night. Everybody thought that's why he did it, out of hate, but it wasn't. He could care less what she did in the bedroom. He liked her and how she walked tough and talked tougher. He'd just gotten so damn sick of looking at that house, and of it blocking the light from his uncle's porch. Everything was so damn close together in town, he couldn't breathe right. Plus, his mama had always said that sunlight was the best cure for anything that doctors couldn't, and since Dill wouldn't leave the porch, Leroy figured the only way to get him some sunlight was to get rid of all that blocked it.

She'd swim out towards the thick forest on the far bank, towards the wild, towards her freedom. But always, she would turn back...

He took down the roof over his uncle's porch with a handsaw and a crowbar, the trees with a chainsaw, and the lady's rental house out front with a fire. She'd always rented it to no-goods anyway, pillheads and drunks, like Timmy Wynder, who called Leroy a retard all through school and shoved him into lockers before they'd both dropped out. You'd think a cop wouldn't want to rent to someone like that, but Leroy figured she needed the money just like everybody else.

Timmy had gone to jail about a week before Leroy did it, left the place all trashed and stinking. It's not like he'd wanted to hurt somebody. It's not like he planned to do something bad. How do you explain something like that? He knew it didn't make sense to anyone. He knew it was stupid too, knew that as soon as he lit the match. That's all he could say to the judge. He didn't say that fire's got a powerful pull, but that's true too. He'd spent seven years on house arrest working odd jobs for mechanics around town. Midway through his time the lady cop had hired him to rebuild the house. She'd paid him and everything. He couldn't believe that. She knew he'd burnt it down—everybody knows everything in a town that size—but she hired him anyway, didn't seem to hold a grudge against him.

■ ■ ■

When he got back to the car, his woman was still red faced, but now she was awake and mad too.

"What the hell took you so long?"

He said nothing.

"We're outta food."

He handed her a bag with a liter of water, two Cokes, some Fritos, a Snickers, and an Oatmeal Cream Pie hanging heavy inside, and said, "They didn't have no Mountain Dew." The baby cried. She stuck her knuckle in his mouth to try to quiet him, but he was hot and madder even than she.

"Hope you can fix it fast, Leroy! Maybe if you'd got a better job we wouldn't be driving this piece of trash all the way to Texas!" She kicked the passenger door, and he heard her say it under her breath, "Dumbass can't even read, how the hell's he gonna feed us three?"

Then she turned on her heel, and walked a ways down the road to the nearest telephone pole. She sat down in the thin shadow that sliced across the grass between the highway and the rice field. It took him the rest of the evening to get the car fixed, and she didn't come back until she heard the engine start. By then it was near dark.

They slept in the car that night. She and the baby in the backseat. He could hear her snoring gently. He sat in the front, careful not to recline too far back and disturb them. The traffic died down somewhere in the early hours of morning, but even still the whine of tractor trailers was a constant, like the river back home.

Leroy must have dozed, because when he awoke to the sun breaking across the horizon, no hills or trees to block it, he found himself at the intersection of relief and sadness. Sad because it had only been a dream and the lion was not in the backseat behind him, staring calmly out the windshield as if monitoring his driving. And relieved because there were no sirens and lights close behind. No nauseating guilt that he had left his wife and the baby back there on the side of the road.

There were just the starlings, hundreds of them, maybe thousands, gathered along the phone lines that crossed the rice fields and highway perpendicularly. His old lady didn't wake up until they were a good ways past Little Rock. The sun was still low in the sky, fat clouds way up in the blue heavens above, and finally a sign that he knew how to read—cause she'd taught him to in the letters her mama sent—that read *Texarkana, 89 miles.* ■

BLOSSOMING INDIGO

I coveted the Wranglers my brother wore
when we played outside—durable denim
seat impervious to rocks, sticks, glass shards
unearthed when we scooted toward the stream,
worn knees grass-dyed lucent chartreuse,
pockets deep enough to hold his morning finds—
bumboozers, bottlecaps, buckeyes—treasure
I had to secure in the dirty hem of my skirt—
what "ladies" wore to church, to play, to school
where other girls arrived each September
in Lees with pleats and pink pinstripes.
But they're pink! My rebuttal when my father
defended his edict with Deuteronomy 22:5,
declared jeans are for boys, refused
even my plea to try on one pair, just to see,
to take on each lean leg like I'd watched
my friends do, ease them over calves, knees,
shimmy past thighs, hips, around my waist;
look over my shoulder; discover curves
blossoming indigo; a woman in the glass
reflecting why he always said no.

CATHERINE PRITCHARD CHILDRESS

BEYOND THE ROPE

He pressed his face against canvas
ignoring signs marked *Do Not Touch,*
zooming in, with one bright iris,
on primary colors and shapes.

Shading him from the docent's view,
I guided his fingers with mine
as he brushed the raised acrylic—
oiled red monochrome of apples,
barn, incongruous sails atop
hand-hewn canoes floating downstream
between log cabins and tall pines.

I described windows of churches—
Holding his fingertips steady,
traced straight lines of rectangled frames,
sketched curves of intricate stained glass,
leaned in close as he discovered
the rendering of wood and stone.

He asked me to read every word
written beside each vivid scene—
to repeat these lines:
                                        "She's a tree
of life to them who can lay hold
upon her"
                wondered why no "she"
appeared in the painted landscape

he could see only when his hands,
held tightly in my own, reached out;
yielded to my pressure; stroked trees,
revealing fruit—his eyes open.

CATHERINE PRITCHARD CHILDRESS

BOOK REVIEWS

Amy Greene. *Long Man: A Novel.* New York, N.Y.: Knopf, 2014. 288 pages. Hardcover. $25.95.

Reviewed by Jesse Graves

In her much-anticipated second novel *Long Man,* Amy Greene takes up the challenge of creating a fictional account of the removal of citizens from their homes by the Tennessee Valley Authority (TVA) in the mid-1930s. No other cultural event affected so many lives in rural East Tennessee, which is the setting of Greene's novel. The debate about the TVA remains unresolved after nearly eighty years, and recent incidents such as the coal ash spill of 2008 in Kingston, Tennessee, serve as reminders of the source of resistance to the institution. Was TVA a case of egregious government intrusion on private lives and private property, or

was it a necessary sacrifice by some for the good of the many, a manageable consequence of progress for the common good? These issues are tangible in Greene's novel, but such political questions are present without overwhelming her attention to the characters and their experiences, which make *Long Man* such a memorable piece of writing.

Though many compelling characters populate *Long Man*, the presence of Annie Clyde Dodson dominates the novel. She is an independent young woman who lives with her husband and small daughter on the farm she inherited from her deceased parents. TVA agents fear her, and neighbors—before they left the condemned town of Yuneetah—seemed mostly confounded by her. She is not friendly or charming, not witty or eloquent. She is more like a force of nature; solitary, mindful, and above all, powerful. Her independence is all the more remarkable given the time and place in which the novel is set, and in her role as a married woman at odds with her husband about their future.

The character who most balances the novel, and provides a kind of antithesis to Annie Clyde Dodson, is a drifter named Amos who was raised in Yuneetah and returns to find it almost completely empty. Amos's motives are unclear from the beginning, just as Annie Clyde's motives—to remain on her land so that her daughter may experience the beauty and freedom of that world—are perfectly clear. Amos is a man without articulate convictions, yet definitely drawn toward some unspoken goal in his trip back through the abandoned town of his youth. The new TVA dam, which has driven most everyone else away from the town, seems to have pulled Amos back toward it.

Greene very subtly introduces the major dramatic event of the novel with an intensely gripping scene in which Annie Clyde and James Dodson slowly realizes that their child, Gracie, has disappeared. Tension is built steadily as scene after scene shows the water rising in Yuneetah, with the Dodsons waiting until the last day to evacuate before it reaches dangerous levels. A real sense of panic instills the first pages of Gracie's disappearance and the foggy and rainy nighttime search that ensues. Annie Clyde incriminates Amos, and some of the interesting secondary characters, like her difficult aunt, Silver Ledford—who leads an isolated life as a bootlegger higher up in the ridges above Yuneetah—begin to play important roles.

Greene avoids sentimentality, without sacrificing sentiment. Long Man brings a world long past back into existence, and fills it with characters and situations that are as complex as the world today.

None of the characters in *Long Man* are exactly likeable in any conventional way, except the child Gracie and faithful hound Rusty. This presents another remarkable aspect of the book: Greene avoids sentimentality, without sacrificing sentiment. *Long Man* brings a world long past back into existence, and fills it with characters and situations that are as complex as the world today.

Certain readers will likely feel they have seen one too many lonely old granny women in mountain cabins who have a special "second sight," or one too many beaten-down but good-hearted sheriffs in Appalachian fiction. Somewhere out there, an industrious graduate student surely is writing a dissertation called *Conflicted Lawmen in American Fiction,* and Greene's Ellard Moody would deserve a chapter alongside

Cormac McCarthy's Ed Tom Bell from *No Country for Old Men* and Ron Rash's Will Alexander from *One Foot in Eden.* Moody could easily have been a flat character, or one that most readers have seen before, but in *Long Man,* the sheriff's devotion is not automatic, not assumed. He remains steadily unsure if he is doing anyone any good, and his nemesis Amos (whom Moody misreads, largely for personal reasons), certainly feels that Moody has failed the town he has sworn to protect. Such fine shadings prevent familiar characters types from feeling like stereotypes.

The same point could be made for Beulah Kesterson, the granny woman in *Long Man.* She is solitary and frightening to the other characters for her "reading of the bones" she wears around her neck, but she also displays warmth and kindness toward the unloved Amos, whom she has raised since he was abandoned in childhood. There are no simple characters, or simple solutions, in *Long Man,* and that is part of what makes it so fascinating.

With *Long Man,* Amy Greene has accomplished the most difficult task of following up her hugely successful first novel *Bloodroot.* As a global bestseller that has been translated into several languages, while simultaneously being embraced in her native Appalachia, *Bloodroot* casts a deep shadow. But *Long Man* surpasses its predecessor in many ways. More sophisticated in style and structure than *Bloodroot,* the novel better sustains its tension and focus, and is more emotionally resonant in its conclusions.

Long Man displays the growth of a serious artist. Greene has been praised for her lyricism, and while that is the quality that stands out most in her writing, *Long Man* develops a new clarity to counterbalance the lyrical beauty of the novel's language, and that makes a potent combination. Greene brings the past into a vivid contemporaneity, writing about lives and struggles that will be impossible for most readers to forget in a voice that is both intense and clear as her Silver Ledford's whiskey. *Long Man* delivers the happy message that one of America's most gifted young novelists is working right here, creating her art in the heart of Appalachia.

Sarah Beth Childers. *Shake Terribly the Earth: Stories from an Appalachian Family.* Athens, Ohio: Ohio University Press, 2013. 224 pages. Trade paperback. $24.95.

Reviewed by Beth Newberry

Shake Terribly the Earth, an essay collection by West Virginian Sarah Beth Childers, captures essentials of the memoir genre and the central Appalachian multi-generational familial experience.

Her prose shines in essays like "Ghost Siblings," which centers on the fascinating subject matter of how the author's family, and her mother in particular, cope with the loss of a child from an ectopic pregnancy. Her mother imagines this child ("'It's a boy,' she breathed... 'God told me his name is Christopher Michael and, my darling Sarah Beth, he looks a lot like you'") at various stages of the author's childhood, on road trips, and at school. One of the rich moments of epiphany in the piece comes when the author recounts her concerns about what will happen when her mother meets Christopher Michael in heaven:

> *"I'm afraid my mom will get to heaven and look for Christopher Michael, and he'll be a girl."*

My friend laughed. He's a man of faith, but not the kind to have a divine revelation on the way to the mailbox. "I think if your mother makes it that far—makes it to Heaven and finds her child—you don't have anything to worry about."

... I believe my mother's going to Heaven, and I believe in my mother, even if the two beliefs sometimes amount to the same thing. I'm not worried about my mother's faith. I worry my mother won't find the person she's expecting, and I fear the revelation will cause her pain.

A clear hallmark of memoir is allowing the reader to experience the author's moments of realization with her as it happens, but it requires a brave writer to share something so raw and unfiltered, and Childers does so without pause. She also excels at dialogue that illuminates her family story, as in "My Dead-Grandmother Essay." Treading through family lore, one's own memories, and those memories retold by kin is a daunting cacophony of perspectives to try to distill into artful writing. Childers does this with varying success in this collection. Small details such as alternating from third person—referring to her parents and grandmother by first names when recounting their relationships with each other—to first person when addressing her own memories or relationships (a storytelling device present throughout the collection) is at times distracting and distances the reader from the story. But by the end, well-crafted scenes, balanced with dialogue and appropriate amount of descriptive detail, smooth over most of the sharp edges.

For example, in the final scene of "My Dead-Grandmother Essay" the narrator describes an intimate moment with her grandmother that is rich in sensory detail and immerses the reader in the moment: “On granny’s rare visits to our house, she smoked outside on the concrete steps that led from the driveway to our back door. When I was four, I sat next to her, my cheek against the polyester blouse, watching the pale gray smoke and the blue-tailed lizards that darted in and out of the cracks between the steps and the brick foundation…Later, alone, I pretended to smoke, puffing on twigs, raking my dull pink nails across my unmarked tongue.” The sensations of touch, sight, and taste elicited in this passage eliminate any distance between narrator and reader, leaving the reader with an all-encompassing feeling of being part of the scene instead of just a witness to it.

The majority of the essays in *Shake Terribly the Earth* show the best of what family memoir can be—the musings, the imaginings, the new perspective on past experiences. Her storytelling skill is also clear in “Scissors,” where three generations of women cope with their mother’s expectations for femininity, religious tradition, and hairstyles. This essay is a collection of many small stories and observations on an object, containing skillful execution of a thematic exploration with stick-with-you dialogue and scene: “My mother pulled into the driveway after a last-minute grocery run, and I raced outside, yelling, ‘She’s got the scissors!’ …At the word ‘scissors,’ my mother left the card door open and strode purposefully through the back door, her brown curls flopping against her shoulders. ‘Where is she?’” In contrast, another essay titled “Through a Train Window” takes the same approach but with less success, feeling more like an exercise in memoir where the pieces of the puzzle felt forced together, and the few false notes overshadowed warmer, heartfelt scenes.

Childers’s collection requires a patient reader to follow all the branches of her family tree in the detailed, descriptive narrative. But for those that join her, it's a rewarding read, a personal history captured in stories that cross generations of a mountain family. ■

BOOK NOTES

Gilbert Allen. *Catma*. Evansville, Ind.: Measure Press, 2014. 93 pages. Hardcover. $20.00.

Allen's latest poetry collection is full of wit, wordplay, and humor. These poems see his poking affectionate fun at rednecks, retirees, religious fanatics, academics, and politicians, to name but a few targets of his wry pen.

John Branscum and Wayne Thomas, editors. *Red Holler: Contemporary Appalachian Literature.* Louisville, Ky.: Sarabande Books, 2013. 256 pages. Trade paperback. $16.95.

This handsome anthology places the span of contemporary Appalachian literature on full display. Fiction, creative nonfiction, poetry, and even graphic narratives are all here, with the work of familiar writers including Ron Rash, Crystal Wilkinson, Karen Salyer McElmurray, and Maurice Manning placed alongside that of emerging voices.

Richard Gilbert. *Shepherd: A Memoir.* East Lansing, Mich.: Michigan State University Press, 2014. 318 Pages. Trade paperback. $24.95

In this thoughtful memoir, Gilbert recounts his decision to move with his family from town to country in Appalachian Ohio, purchasing a farm to breed and sell sheep. But everything is not bucolic—they lose money, their flock faces illness, and Gilbert is haunted by his father's loss of his childhood farm. His family's story of perseverance on the land and among the sheep makes for a poetic homage to rural life and the struggle of chasing a dream.

Leatha Kendrick. *Almanac of the Invisible.* Monterey, Ky.: Larkspur Press, 2014. 52 pages, with illustrations by Arwen Donahue. Paperback. $26.00.

Kentucky poet Kendrick bears witness to love, loss, land, and seasons in this lyrical collection. She offers moving meditations on birdsong and turkey buzzards, the seven ages of Shakespeare, and fighting breast cancer, all alongside exquisite drawings from artist Arwen Donahue.

Builder Levy. *Appalachia USA: Photographs by Builder Levy.* Boston, Mass.: David R. Godine, 2014. 123 pages. Hardcover. $40.00.

These stunning photographs, collected between 1968 and 2009, offer a beautiful, complex, and moving chronicle of the landscape, people, and protest movements of Appalachia.

Laura Long. *Out of Peel Tree: A Novel.* Morgantown, W. Va.: West Virginia University Press, 2014. 140 pages. Trade paperback. $16.99.

Billed as a novel in stories, Long's *Out of Peel Tree* chronicles moments in the lives of a scattered mountain family: the runaway delinquent who is trying to build a life in Texas, a parolee on his way to Reno, Nevada, a woman who receives a letter that changes everything. The layered writing and use of sensory details make this debut a pleasure—and this author one to watch.

Paulette Livers. *Cementville.* Berkley, Calif.: Counterpoint Press, 2014. 304 pages. Trade paperback. $19.95.

Set in a small Kentucky town in 1969, *Cementville* opens with the bodies of a local group of dead soldiers returning home from Vietnam. The collective grief felt by the townspeople leads to something more—a sense of community, along with mysterious acts of violence. In her debut novel, Livers skillfully depicts a town attempting to reconcile tradition with an approaching new order.

Roger May. *Testify: Photographs by Roger May*. Durham, N.C.: Horse & Buggy Press, 2014. 72 pages in two volumes, and a foreword by Silas House. Fine press book. $65.00.

May's unflinching eye captures Appalachia from the perspective of both insider and outsider in this profound collection of photographs. *Testify* records a personal journey of home and family—and all their complexities.

Emma Bell Miles. *Once I Too Had Wings: The Journals of Emma Bell Miles, 1908-1918.* Steven Cox, Editor. Athens, Ohio: Ohio University Press, 2014. 352 pages with index, foreword by Elizabeth Engelhardt and list of illustrations. Trade paperback. $28.95.

At the turn of the twentieth-century, Emma Bell Miles's prose often graced the pages of magazines such as *Harper's Weekly,* and her nonfiction book *The Spirit of the Mountains* offered a complex portrait of mountain life. But her own world was often troubled. These writings, expertly collected by Cox, delve into Miles's life and observations on her family's challenging economic circumstances, her son's death from scarlet fever, and her own fight against tuberculosis, all transcribed in her trademark evocative prose.

Rita Quillen. *Hiding Ezra.* Johnson City, Tenn.: Little Creek Books, 2014. 220 pages. Trade paperback. $12.95.

When the United States is pulled into World War I, Ezra Teague, a farmer from southwest Virginia, faces a choice: loyality to his country or his family. Choosing the latter, he goes on the run for two years to escape military prosecution. Poet Quillen's debut novel is full of drama and beautifully told.

Jon Sealy. *The Whiskey Baron: A Novel.* Spartanburg, S.C.: Hub City Press, 2014. 250 pages. Trade paperback. $18.99.

I've had choices since the day I was born, George Jones once sang, a lyric that could be used to describe the plot of Sealy's highly readable debut novel. When two men are shot and killed outside a boardinghouse in South Carolina in 1932, the local sheriff must investigate. Clues point him toward the head of the local bootlegging operation, setting up a clash of small town powers.

Joe Survant. *The Land We Dreamed: Poems.* Lexington, Ky.: University Press of Kentucky, 2014. 148 pages. Trade paperback. $19.95.

In the final volume of his trilogy of poetry collections on rural Kentucky, Survant explores the frontier history of the Commonwealth. Each poem takes the reader on an adventure with characters including Dr. Thomas Walker, Daniel Boone, and chiefs of the Shawnee and Seneca tribes.

Jacinda Townsend. *Saint Monkey*. New York, N.Y.: W.W. Norton & Company, Inc., 2014. 288 pages. Hardcover. $24.95.

Set in rural Kentucky and New York City during the 1950s, this compelling debut novel follows the intertwining lives of two African-American women whose friendship is strained by distance, resentment, family, and hope deferred. Exploring classic themes of home and exile, Townsend's novel is a must-read.

YOUNG ADULT

Sarah Combs. *Breakfast Served Anytime*. Somerville, Mass.: Candlewick Books, 2014. 272 pages. Hardcover. $16.99.

A summer spent at "geek camp" among gifted misfits is the subject of Combs's moving debut. Gloria, a rising high school senior from rural Kentucky, is mourning the loss of her grandmother when she arrives at the camp. Her quartet of friends roam the grounds and savor breakfast all day at a local restaurant, sharing a magical summer that leaves them forever changed.

Tommy Hays. *What I Came to Tell You*. New York, N.Y.: EgmontUSA, 2013. 304 pages. Hardcover. $16.99

Grover is a sensitive young boy struggling to come to terms with the loss of his mother in a tragic accident. As his sister and father deal with the grief in their own ways, Grover submerges himself in crafting weavings from leaves and branches. *What I Came to Tell You* is an aching story about the healing power of art and family. ■

CONTRIBUTORS

Rob Amberg is a photographer from Madison County, North Carolina. He has received fellowships from the National Endowment for the Arts, National Endowment for the Humanities, and the John Simon Guggenheim Memorial Foundation. His first book, *Sodom Laurel Album,* received the Thomas Wolfe Literary Award of the Western North Carolina Historical Association. Find out more about Amberg and his work at www.robamberg.com.

Catherine Pritchard Childress lives in East Tennessee where she teaches writing and literature at East Tennessee State University and Northeast State Community College. Her work has appeared or is forthcoming in *North American Review, Louisiana Literature, Connecticut Review, Still: The Journal, The Cape Rock, Town Creek Poetry, drafthorse, Stoneboat, Kaimana,* and *Kudzu,* and has been anthologized in *The Southern Poetry Anthology, Volume VI: Tennessee.*

David Cornette is a 2014 graduate from Berea College, where he earned a Bachelor of Arts in English Literature. While a student at Berea, he worked as an editor for *Apollon: The Undergraduate Ejournal,* as well as an assistant for *Appalachian Heritage.* He is currently interning with Grow Appalachia at the Hindman Settlement School and has a publication forthcoming in *Still: The Journal.*

Kevin Gardner has received numerous awards for his art, which has been exhibited in solo and group shows nationally. Primarily a painter, his work is mostly perceptual and is frequently inspired by historic work. He holds a Certificate in Painting from the Pennsylvania Academy of the Fine Arts and an MFA in Painting from Indiana University-Bloomington. Gardner is currently an Assistant Professor of Painting and Drawing at Berea College.

Rachel Garringer lives a stone's throw from the sheep farm where she was raised in southeastern West Virginia. When not writing fiction she works as a youth advocate, interviews rural and small town LGBTQI folks for an oral history project called *Country Queers,* and spends as much time as possible out in the garden and the woods. "Vultures," which appeared in the Fall 2013 issue of *Still: The Journal,* was her first published work.

Denise Giardina is the author of six novels including the national bestsellers *Storming Heaven, The Unquiet Earth,* and most recently, *Emily's Ghost.* She lives in Charleston, West Virginia.

Carol Grametbauer writes poetry in Kingston, Tennessee, where she is chair of the board of directors of Tennessee Mountain Writers. Her poems have appeared in *Appalachian Heritage, POEM, The Cabinet, The Kerf, Still: The Journal, Fluent,* and *Maypop*; and in *The Southern Poetry Anthology, Volume VI: Tennessee* and *Remember September: Prompted Poetry*. Her chapbook, *Now & Then,* was released by Finishing Line Press in March 2014.

Jesse Graves is the author of two poetry collections, *Tennessee Landscape with Blighted Pine,* and *Basin Ghosts,* and is co-editor of three volumes of the Southern Poetry Anthology series, including a forthcoming collection of North Carolina poets. He is also working with Dr. Michael Lofaro to edit *The Collected Poems of James Agee.*

Michael Henson is author of three books of fiction and four collections of poetry. His most recent work is *The True Story of the Resurrection and Other Poems* from Wind Publications. He is co-editor of *Pine Mountain Sand & Gravel,* the annual publication of the Southern Appalachian Writers Cooperative.

Janice Hornburg is a native Texan who transplanted to East Tennessee in 1993. Her chapbook, *Perspectives,* was released by Finishing Line Press in 2013. Her work has been anthologized in the *Anthology of Appalachian Writers, Volume V* and *The Southern Poetry Anthology, Vol. VI: Tennessee,* and has appeared in *Appalachian Heritage, Chapter 16, Town Creek Poetry,* and *Tennessee Voices.*

Karen Salyer McElmurray's *Surrendered Child: A Birth Mother's Journey,* was an AWP Award Winner for Creative Nonfiction. Her novels are *The Motel of the Stars* and *Strange Birds in the Tree of Heaven.* Other stories and essays have appeared in *Iron Horse, Kenyon Review, Alaska Quarterly Review,* and *River Teeth,* and have been widely anthologized. In Spring 2014, she was the Louis Rubin Writer-in-Residence at Hollins University.

Jim Minick is the author of four books, most recently *The Blueberry Years,* winner of the Best Nonfiction Book of the Year from Southern Independent Booksellers Association. He teaches at Converse College and is the Fred Chappell Fellow at University of North Carolina-Greensboro, where he is pursuing an MFA.

Rachel Morgan is the Assistant Poetry Editor for the *North American Review* and teaches creative writing at the University of Northern Iowa. She co-edited *Fire Under the Moon: An Anthology of Contemporary Slovene Poetry* (Black Dirt Press). Recently her work appears or is forthcoming in *Fence, Denver Quarterly, Barely South, Volt, Hunger Mountain, South85,* and *DIAGRAM.*

R.C. Neighbors is a sixth-generation Oklahoman who has studied literature at the University of Arkansas and creative writing at Hollins University. He is currently completing his Ph.D. at Texas A&M University with an emphasis in Native Southern studies and creative writing. His work has appeared or is forthcoming in *Tampa Review, Barely South Review, Red Earth Review,* and *Parody.*

Beth Newberry is a writer and editor living in Louisville, Kentucky. Her work has been published in *Sojourners, Still: The Journal,* and *The Louisville Review.* Her essay "The Center of the Compass" was named a notable essay of 2010 by Robert Atwan in the 2011 *Best American Essays.* She writes at thehillville.com.

Matt Prater is a poet and writer from Saltville, Virginia. A graduate of Radford University and Appalachian State University, his work has appeared, or is forthcoming, in *Still: The Journal, Now and Then: The Appalachian Magazine, The Hollins Critic,* and the *Motif* anthology series, among other publications.

Jackie White Rogers served for many years as an English teacher in Pulaski County, Kentucky, and now works as a literacy consultant with the Kentucky Department of Education. A writer and photographer, her short fiction and essays have been published in magazines such as *The Louisville Review, Now and Then,* and *Wind,* as well as anthologies. A native of Science Hill, Kentucky, she presently lives in Frankfort.

Carter Sickels is the author of the novel *The Evening Hour*, a finalist for the 2013 Oregon Book Award, the Lambda Literary Debut Fiction Award, and the Publishing Triangle Edmund White Debut Fiction Award. Sickels is the recipient of the 2013 Lambda Literary Emerging Writer Award. He currently teaches in the Low Residency MFA Program at West Virginia Wesleyan University, and lives in Portland, Oregon.

Lora Smith currently serves as communications officer for the Mary Reynolds Babcock Foundation where she works on issues of poverty, economic development, and racial equity in the southern United States. A native of Corbin, Kentucky, she holds a B.A. from New York University and regularly writes for *Punch* magazine and the Southern Foodways Alliance.

Charles Dodd White was born in Atlanta, Georgia, and grew up in both the city and the woods. He has been a Marine, a fishing guide, and a journalist. The recepient of the Jean Ritchie Fellowship, he is the author of the novels *A Shelter of Others* and *Lambs of Men*, the short story collection *Sinners of Sanction County*, and co-editor of the contemporary Appalachian short story anthology *Degrees of Separation*. He currently lives in Candler, North Carolina.